GULZA

Angoor

SATHYA SARAN is the author of critically acclaimed and bestselling biographies of Guru Dutt, S.D. Burman and Jagjit Singh. Her most recent publications are *How to Look like Miss India* (Juggernaut, 2018), and *Knot for Keeps: Writing the Modern Marriage* (HarperCollins India, 2018), an anthology on marriage. Sathya, who was editor of the first women's magazine of India, *Femina*, for twelve years, is currently a Consulting Editor with HarperCollins Publishers India and teaches fashion journalism at the National Institute of Fashion Technology (NIFT). She also conceptualized and curates 'The Spaces between Words: The Unfestival' sponsored by JSW and *The Hindu*.

Among her many accolades are several national awards, the Roshni TIA Inspirational Woman Award 2018, the Bharat Nirman (1996), the Young Journalist Award (1994), and the Mahila Shiromani Award, presented by the First Lady of India, for her contribution to journalism.

GULZAR'S
Angoor

INSIGHTS INTO THE FILM

SATHYA SARAN

HarperCollins *Publishers* India

First published in India by
HarperCollins *Publishers* in 2019
A-75, Sector 57, Noida, Uttar Pradesh 201301, India
www.harpercollins.co.in

2 4 6 8 10 9 7 5 3 1

P-ISBN: 978-93-5302-512-0
E-ISBN: 978-93-5302-513-7

Typeset in 11.5/15 Bembo at
Manipal Digital Systems, Manipal

Printed and bound at
Thomson Press (India) Ltd

To a Bard who set the ball rolling.
And a poet who picked it up and changed it into
a bunch of grapes!

Contents

ॐ

CONTENTS

Preface

CR

Ask me to choose between a comedy and a tragedy, and I will go straight for the latter. Tragedies are thought-provoking; they delve into human nature, the failings and foibles of great and small people. Tragedies show us our weaknesses and warn us of the pitfalls that await even those who have achieved greatness. Comedies, on the other hand, make us laugh, sweep us into a long moment of forgetfulness, delivering an opiate for the senses from the travails of daily living. And when they are done, the reality is twice as hard. Tragedies, on the other hand, make you realize that indeed all the world is a stage, and your problems are small compared to what befell those on screen or stage. They also give you insights into how relationships develop, change, turn sour, and ... oh come on, tragedies teach a lot. Comedies, well, as I said before, they just make you laugh.

Which is why when, of the three books chosen to present Gulzar's cinema, I was presented with *Angoor*, I baulked a little. I was thrilled to be working on a book on Gulzar's film, being one among his legion of fans, but *Angoor* ... hmm. I had watched the film, it was funny, I remembered. But really, I would have preferred *Ijaazat*. So nuanced a film, such a compelling story, such music, and then there was the visual poetry that added to the actors' craft. Yes, if given a choice, *Ijaazat* it would have been.

But the die had been cast, and *Angoor* it was. I took the assignment and carried it off like a prize, a consolation prize, but still, one I was happy to have been awarded.

Watching the film at home, I realized that what I thought was gilt was indeed gold. Here was comedy that was not just a series of funny moments strung together. Here was one master artist working on the material created by the master of all craftsmen, Shakespeare, and making it all his own. When the film ended, I sat back, leaned forward and started it all over again, realizing by now, that there were so many layers in the film that needed attention. Suddenly, comedy held a new meaning. I took a deep breath and prepared to take the full measure of what I had on hand.

Everything about *Angoor* is worth paying attention to. Almost every gesture, every line of dialogue or song has a reason for being. It is tightly knit, unlike most comedies, except for a few exceptions, which, in my mind primarily include *Chalti ka Naam Gaadi, Jaane Bhi Do Yaaro, Chupke Chupke*, and *Gol Maal*. Incidentally, the last two are also written by Gulzar.

Angoor kept me quite busy. A major handicap was that Sanjeev Kumar was no longer around, and Deven Verma was too ill to give me audience when I called, and passed away before I could ask again. Moushumi Chatterjee would only speak to me on the phone, and her information was sketchy at best. It remained for Deepti Naval and Gulzar to fill in the main actors' parts too, and give me enough about their approach to their roles. Happily for me, both filled the need most adequately. Besides, insights from director Debu Sen and actress Tanuja helped shed light on the behind-the-scenes action in *Do Dooni Char*.

Shantanu Ray Chaudhuri, who was my editor when I started the book, gave me the idea of also delineating the history of comedy in Hindi cinema to be able to give *Angoor* a proper setting. That chapter, I think will also help readers understand the highly evolved humour of *Angoor*, that has the capacity to entertain anyone from eight-year-olds onwards. In fact, at every decade of his life, the viewer will discover new meanings to the lines.

Writing the book has been fun. It took me back to my student days when as a student of literature I had to take apart a book, a play or some piece of writing to understand it, critique it and present it so others would get the most of the original, thanks to my interpretation.

So, dear reader, that is what this book tries to do. To unravel the craft of the writer, demystify the craft of the filmmaker, present the value of enjoyment that the lyrics and music add, all of which when combined by the actors' genius in comic timing, makes for great viewing. My challenge was to keep it light and fun, and not make the book into a dissertation. I think I have managed that!

A good script lies at the heart of every good film. Writing comedy is so much tougher than writing tragedy. Tragedy presents itself at every turn. Comedy hides in secret places, and only the sharpest eye and keenest mind can discover and reveal it. Thanks to *Angoor*, I know this.

If after reading this book, you decide to watch *Angoor* again, I know I have risen to the task. Be sure you sit around with the entire family to watch the film. It is a great bonding device!

chapter one

Tales from Shakespeare

CR

It all began with Shakespeare.

Of course there are many versions of the possible dates and chronology of Shakespeare's plays. But the Encylopedia Britannica states that his much loved comedy, *The Comedy of Errors,* was the Bard's fourth creation, coming on the heels of *The Two Gentlemen of Verona, Love's Labour Lost,* and *Henry VI Part One* and, *Titus Andronicus.* Critics were of course still watching the new playwright closely, and found it fit to label the play 'an apprentice comedy'. Despite the criticism, Shakespeare put up the play on the Feast of the Holy Innocents, on 28 December 1594, at the Gray's Inn Christmas Revels to a learned audience of lawyers and aspirants to the legal profession, who found it entertaining despite the slapstick elements, that were quite a departure from the playwright's earlier works. In fact, the play contributed to the rowdy Christmas celebrations, as recorded in the *Gesta Grayorum* published in 1688. Established as a play perfect for Christmas revels, it was performed again at Court in 1604, when 'The Plaie of Errors', by 'Shaxberd' was staged by His Majesty's Players.

As anyone who has studied Shakespeare knows, most of his stories were based on either an older, classical tale, or were an amalgamation of many such stories. This would be true in the case of his most famous plays like *Hamlet, Prince of Denmark* and *Macbeth,* and was true too of *The Comedy of Errors,* which is reportedly based on *Menaechmi,* a Roman comedy written by the ancient dramatist Plautus who lived between 254–184 BC, which Shakespeare read as an English translation in the late 1590s.

Though the play must have excited his fancy, Shakespeare improved on it, adding elements from his own imagination, or possibly from other writings he had read, including another play by Plautus, titled *Amphitruo.* He added a second set of twins, married one off, and thus created a canvas that had enough scope for twists and turns that would confound and mystify the audience even as it gave rise to situations that could have them splitting their sides laughing at the innumerable misunderstandings arising out of mistaken identities. Keeping in mind that he had to mix the new with the familiar to hold the audience's interest, he added the tried and tested laughter-inducing shrewish wife who was a constant character in English comedies of that time.

The mix worked well. Audiences roared with laughter through the scenes and came back for repeats. And repeats became a common occurrence where the play was concerned, spanning not just the years of his career, but centuries beyond the Bard's time.

Though it was titled *See If You Like It,* the play staged in Covent Garden in 1734 was an obvious adaptation of Shakespeare's comedy. Less than ten years later, in 1741, Drury Lane had a new version with a star performer playing a major role – an indication of the popularity of the play and the company's faith that it would earn enough to justify the star performer's fees. The most successful adapter was Thomas Hull. He added songs and many romantic scenes to the original to his version titled *The Twins,* which had successful runs at Covent Garden through the latter half of the eighteenth century and some years of the early nineteenth century too.[1] Centuries later, in the 1980s, the Flying Karamazov Brothers adapted the play in a manner that was quite their own, adding jugglers and a veritable circus into the shows at the Lincoln Center in New York, which was shown on MTV and PBS.[2]

---

1 See rsc.org.uk

2 PBS or the Public Broadcasting Service is an American public broadcaster and distributor, a non-profit organization providing educational programmes to public TV stations in the US.

Shakespeare's play resurfaced as an opera in 1786, delighting audiences at the Burgtheater in Vienna. Titled *Gli Equivoci*, the opera was closely fashioned after a French translation of the original play.

Another operatic version went on stage in 1819, with the music credits shared by Mozart, among others. And in 1855, Samuel Phelps delved into the original script of the play and staged it at Sadler's Wells Theatre.

Musical productions, too, mined the play and *The Boys from Syracuse* (1938) was the first version, with Richard Rodgers and Lorenz Hart scoring the music. In 1976, Trevor Nunn's version for the Royal Shakespeare Company, with a score by Guy Woolfenden, won the Laurence Olivier Award for best musical. Nunn would also script the TV adaptation of the play. In 1981, the play was adapted again, titled *Oh, Brother!*, with a score written by Michael Valenti and Donald Driver.[3]

Late in 2001, *The Bomb-itty of Errors*, a hip-hop version, 'part play, part rap concert,' won the Grand Jury first prize at HBO's Comedy Festival.

Cinema borrowed freely from the original as well. Following Shakespeare's penchant for giving classics a twist, the producers of *Big Business* (1988) had Bette Milder and

---

3   Robert S. Moila and Philip C. Kolin (eds), 'Comedy of Errors', in *Critical Essays*, New York, London: Psychology Press, Garland Publishing Inc., 1997.

Lily Tomlin play the female twins in a version of the play. And, in 1978, a production of *The Comedy of Errors* was launched in the then USSR.

In fact, even with its many avatars, the play still holds its own. At Chicago's Old Globe Theatre, the publicity announcement reads: 'William Shakespeare's "The Comedy of Errors" – a classic farce of furious wives and confused mistresses retold with a jazz twist – opened Saturday at The Old Globe.' And a news write-up adds: 'Tony and Emmy Award nominee Scott Ellis makes his directorial debut at the Globe in this 2015 Summer Shakespeare Festival production on the outdoor stage.' The only major change made to the play was that the Globe production exchanged the ancient Greek city of Ephesus for 1920s' New Orleans and mined the jazz music of the era to add an extra punch to the play.

Of course, the world's largest film producers could not be left behind; India has six versions of this Shakespearean play. In languages as varied as Bangla, Punjabi, Hindi and Tulu, the humour of the uniquely hilarious situations created by Shakespeare has found expression. *Ulta Palta* (1997) was a film in Kannada, while *Aamait Asal Eemait Kusal* (2012) was produced in Tulu. *Double Di Trouble*, released just five years ago in 2014, had Punjabi audiences laughing at the misadventures of Dharmendra, who played one of the twin protagonists.

But it was Ishwar Chandra Vidyasagar who really set the ball rolling. In 1869, he adapted the play in Bangla and published it under the title *Bhranti Bilash*, as part of his endeavour to popularize Shakespeare and the Romantics and add strength to the Renaissance in Bengal. And when the book was used as the base for a film of the same name in 1963, starring matinee idol Uttam Kumar, Shakespeare formally arrived in Indian cinema; the Hindi versions, *Do Dooni Char* (1968) and *Angoor* (1982), would follow in due course.

chapter two

Gulzar Sees the Thriller

A Story

ॐ

Gulzar called *A Comedy of Errors* a thriller.

That is one way of looking at it. Actually, Shakespeare's play has all the ingredients of a thriller. There is crime; there is suspense, theft and punishment; there is even the threat of one of the characters losing his head at the climax of the story! And then there is romance and mystery.

Shake all these ingredients and you can pull out a number of angles and approaches from the same mix.

Shakespeare chose to stir the mix with a strong dose of humour. Cashing in on the element of confusion arising out of two sets of twins with not just the same faces but also the same names, he pushed the rest of the elements into the background. Thus though the ingredients are all present, the thriller element is only a backdrop to set the laughs into and keep the story moving forward.

Shakespeare's story starts, like many of his other ones, with a dramatic opening. A Syracuse merchant named Egeon is condemned to die for breaking a law that forbids citizens of the rival city from entering Ephesus. He begs for reprieve even as he is being led to his death. The story he narrates is astounding enough to make the Duke stop to listen.

Egeon tells the Duke and the audience that he had ventured into Ephesus in the hope of finding his wife and one of his twin sons, whom he had lost in a shipwreck twenty-five years ago. The twin who he brought up is also travelling through cities, searching for his lost brother, and both twins have twin brothers as servants. Convinced that the man is telling him the truth, despite the seeming impossibility of the story, the Duke gives him a day's reprieve. However, he will be executed as planned if he fails to procure the required ransom of a thousand marks by the next day.

Coincidentally, the lost son does live in Ephesus and is a rich merchant with a beautiful wife who has a penchant for good jewellery and other fine things in life. To add further spice, the other twin, Antipholus, and his servant too come to the same city. The inevitable happens: the wife of the prosperous twin mistakes her brother-in-law for her husband, drags him home and to ensure privacy tells his servant, Dromio, not to let anyone into the house at any cost. Naturally, when the right husband returns, he is not allowed entry.

Matters get further tangled when the Ephesusian twin's sister-in-law floats into the sights of the Syracusian twin and he falls in love with her. Shakespeare must have laughed into his sleeve at introducing this seemingly incestuous twist.

With every twist, the skein of the story tangles further. A much-awaited gold necklace, the bone of contention between the Ephesusian twin and his wife, is finally ready and the jeweller mistakes the Syracusian twin for his brother and gives him the chain. When he demands money for the goods later, it is from the wrong twin, who asserts loudly that he has not received the necklace at all. Upset, and sure that her husband is going mad, the wife locks him in the cellar.

When the Syracusian twin and his servant decide to leave what they believe is a land possessed by demons, they are apprehended by the debt officer. They manage to find refuge in an abbey. Further twists in the story create more openings for comedy. The wife approaches the Duke to seek his help to get her husband out from his sanctuary in the abbey, so she can take him home and deal with him in a suitable manner. The real husband, managing to escape from the cellar, also brings a sore complaint to the Duke about his wife's errant behaviour towards him. After giving full rein to the situation and the confusion, which the audience enjoys thoroughly, the mystery is solved. The Abbess produces the twins hiding in her abbey and delivers the final surprise that she is the long-lost mother of one set of twins and the wife of the merchant.

So, it all ends well and everyone pardons everyone else for misdeeds that were genuinely the result of misunderstandings.

So much happens in the course of a single day that the audience is amused, confused and, finally, relieved that everything is sorted out satisfactorily.

Despite lacking much of Shakespeare's introspective profundity that marked most of his later work, *A Comedy of Errors* remains a favourite up to this day.

chapter three

Bhranti Bilash

ର

Since the success of his film *Agni Pariksha* in 1954, Uttam Kumar had grown in stature in the world of Bengali cinema. His on-screen romantic pairing with Suchitra Sen was on its way to becoming legendary, but the star also had other important leading ladies acting opposite him.

Almost a century after Ishwar Chandra Vidyasagar wrote *Bhranti Bilash*, Uttam Kumar took up the story for his film. Naturally, he had also turned producer and *Bhranti Bilash* (as the film was named later) is considered one of his most successful productions. Manu Sen was handed the director's baton.

Though he would start taking up character roles later in the 1960s, in *Bhranti Bilash*, Bengal's most loved hero decided to double his appeal and play the twin roles himself. With Bhanu Bandopadhyay as his foil in both roles and

Sandhya Roy as his wife in one, the star was all set to ensure the film ran to full houses. The presence of much loved actresses like Sabitri Chatterjee and Sabita Bose added to the appeal of the film.

The formula worked effectively, backed by Shakespeare's comic story and Vidyasagar's localized retelling of it with familiar phrases, characterizations and situations. Keeping public taste in mind, the film added a few songs into the story line and Shyamal Mitra's melodies sat well on the persona of the effervescent sister-in-law. Adding the right touch to the ending, the film paired the single twin with the sister-in-law, thus welding the family into a closer unit and tying all loose ends neatly. All was well that ended well.

Indeed, the film did amazingly well and Uttam Kumar looked immaculate as he dominated the screen in his two roles. Though the actor was known and admired for his natural acting style, he put himself out by trying to portray the two different twins and, doffing a cap to the less astute in the audience (for the somewhat dim-witted, it was an obvious differentiation), one twin does carry the snuff-taking mannerism to rather unnecessary lengths.

A puppet show and slapstick comedy might have been aimed at the less urbane or adult audience, but those who flocked to the cinema halls to watch *Bhranti Bilash* would take it all in, and laugh at every twist in the story.

If there was a sly hint of an incestuous attraction on the part of the sister-in-law for her sister's husband, it was left to the audience's imagination and was neatly rounded off by delivering the unmarried twin to her as a perfect match.

Bhranti Bilash had another important role to play in the history of Indian cinema; years after its release, its success and story line would inspire a spin-off in Hindi. Directed by Debu Sen, written by Gulzar and produced under the banner of Bimal Roy Productions, the film would be called *Do Dooni Char.*

chapter four

Behind the Scenes of *Do Dooni Char*

ೞ

The film *Do Dooni Char* was a comedy born of tragedy, or at least an intimation of it.

The year was 1964. Bimal Roy, director and producer of landmark films like *Parineeta* (1953), *Devdas* (1955), *Sujata* (1960) and *Bandini* (1963) was fighting the last stages of lung cancer. It was the desire to keep the banner of Bimal Roy Productions flying despite Roy's debilitated state that motivated the launch of *Do Dooni Char*. The film would be produced and financed by the United Producers, who were also taking care of Bimal Roy's personal comfort and medical and other needs. Bimal Roy's assistant, Debu Sen, was given the responsibility of directing the film. Gulzar, who was also assisting Bimal Roy, was to handle scripting.

Gulzar remembers that Bimal *da* had asked him to work with him to write a film based on the book titled *Amrita*

Kumbher Sandhane by Samaresh Basu. Gulzar believes he was thus chosen because he was anyway on the rolls as a writer of songs and because he was well versed in both Bangla and Hindustani.

Written as a scathing satire under the pen name Kalkut, the narrative was based on a real-life disaster at the Kumbh Mela in 1952 that resulted in the death of more than a 100,000 pilgrims. It was run as a serial in the Bangla newspaper *Ananda Bazar.* Bimal Roy had read the serial, owned a copy of the story published as a novel, and was keen to translate the work into film. 'He was constantly working on it. The book was heavily marked in the margins with his observations,' Gulzar recollects. He also made copious notes that were stuffed into the book at relevant points in the story. In Rinki Roy Bhattacharya's *Bimal Roy: The Man Who Spoke in Pictures*, Gulzar adds, 'The size of the novel was already immense; all those scraps of paper stuffed into it gave it the appearance of a swollen belly – the novel was pregnant with another novel, its binding bursting at the seams. Bimal *da* knew each character so intimately that "*Kumbha*" seemed to be an essential part of his being.'[4]

Bimal Roy made *Bandini* and *Kabuliwala* (1961), even as he pondered over and tackled the larger subject of the Kumbha novel; he also shot a few small scenes for the film,

4   Rinki Bhattacharya (ed.), *Bimal Roy: The Man Who Spoke in Pictures*, Delhi: Penguin Viking, 2009, p. 144.

including fairs, as he preferred the actual colour and sense of the original in a recreation. Gulzar remembers that, in 1963, they were making preparations to shoot the annual Magh Mela at the Sangam in Allahabad and perhaps at the Poorna Kumbh, which would take place two years later in 1965.

As it transpired, Bimal Roy started a high fever that put a sudden end to his plans of shooting in Allahabad. He explained the shots he wanted in great detail, asking the unit to go ahead and shoot so that the fair could be captured. Gulzar remembers that he was coughing a lot, even as he spoke, but it did not stop the director from taking long drags of the Chesterfield cigarette that he favoured.

By the time the unit left for Allahabad, the members knew that Bimal Roy was suffering from cancer. They would come back after faithfully shooting the fair, their hearts heavy with the knowledge, to discover that Bimal Roy had decided to start on a smaller film simultaneously. *Sahara*, as the film was titled, was started while Bimal Roy waited for the Poorna Kumbh to arrive so that he could complete the larger film which he hoped would make him 'a part of the culture of the land'.

Bimal Roy would not live long enough to see the complete script of *Amrita Kumbher Sandhane* but, almost through the fevered phase of his galloping cancer, he worked relentlessly on the script with his writer. Over a period of two months, he would change the time of death of characters every few days, whenever he felt that the character 'dies too early in the narrative', and Gulzar would have to rewrite the scene till he finally found the right timing and scene for the death to be placed. Gulzar says, 'His whole body was racked by coughs but he continued to explain; and when I agreed with him that this was the perfect solution, he looked very enthusiastic and relaxed and promptly asked for a cigarette.'

Through the long months of Bimal Roy's fight with cancer, his office would often remain closed. He had moved home, stating categorically that he 'wanted to die at home', and, for a year, there was no real work done on either of the films he had started. Concerned about his unit and mindful of the need to keep the members active and earning, Bimal Roy decided to find a way to keep the production mill running.

He would entrust Debu Sen with the task he had in mind.

chapter five

Do Dooni Char

The Film that Wasn't

ℭ

The world has forgotten Debu Sen. He lives in a far-flung suburb of Mumbai in a flat that belongs to his son. The days of working with Bimal Roy, the excitement of being an assistant to the great director and of being entrusted a film by him, are all distant memories. Debu Sen today is happy writing poetry and waiting for his grandchild to come home from school.

Knowing his mind to now sometimes cheat him of chronology and facts, Sen has written down every little nugget of memory about the making of *Do Dooni Char* and how the film came into being.

Sen remembers that Roy was shooting a film based on a story titled *Sahara* by Ashapoorna Devi. It starred Dharmendra and Sharmila Tagore in the lead, a very popular screen pairing at that time. Like most of the key members of Bimal Roy Productions, Sen knew that cancer was leaching away the director's life.

'One day Bimal *da* called me,' Sen recollects, 'and said, "17,000 [rupees] have been spent on production of *Sahara* already. So do a cheap, small film. I have spoken to United Producers, and also the Film Finance, and they have approved."' Film Finance was the old National Film Development Corporation of India (NFDC) and the famous poet Premendra Mitra was its President, while Subodh Mukherjee, Mohan Saigal and Hemant Kumar made up United Producers.

Bimal Roy entrusted the writing of the film, based on the Bangla hit *Bhranti Bilash*, to Sen and Birendra Sinha. He added that the Hindi name for the film would be *Do Dooni Char*.

Sen protested, saying that if the film was being made in Hindi, Gulzar should be given the task of writing it. He would be the right person to convert a regional script into one that would appeal to the diverse Hindi-speaking film audiences across the nation.

Gulzar was, thus, officially given the task on hand. Sen remembers that he set about it in right earnest, 'leaving out a number of characters in order to keep the narrative tightly knit. Khayal, also a team member, though not a part of Bimal Roy Productions, transcribed the script in his beautifully crafted Urdu script; 'he would take down notes, too, as we discussed.'

The script was ready in twenty-two days and Sen narrated it to the United Producers. They listened but made no comments. Soon enough, 'We heard from Bimal *da* that it was approved.'

Gulzar has his own memories of the time. 'It was so difficult to write a comedy seeing the state Bimal *da* was in. He had shrunk like a cushion, he coughed incessantly and I would inevitably overhear Sudhendu Roy, who was in charge of art direction, and the cameraman, Kamal Bose, discussing Bimal *da*'s health in Bangla, saying, "It is a matter of days now," or "There is no chance ..." It was impossible to write a song sitting there; I would go home and cry. I could not take it.'

Debu Sen also remembers how broken he felt by Bimal Roy's declining health.

When the writing was done, Sen approached Bimal Roy to ask whom he wanted as director for the film. Sen remembers, 'He was a man of few words, anyway. He kept silent for a while, then said, "You will direct." I got worried [and] asked him, "This is a comedy; can I do it?" He replied, "I have faith that you can." Perhaps he said that because earlier I had written the comedy portions in some scripts. He then said, "Take Dilip Gupta as your cameraman."'

Sen chose Shashi Kapoor and Mehmood to play the main roles. Shashi Kapoor had worked as hero in *Prem Patra* (1962), written by Sen, 'but the film had flopped, so I was bluntly advised to drop the idea. I had no idea of the business end of films, anyway, so did as I was told. Mehmood's price was beyond the sanctioned amount, so we had to look elsewhere.'

'Bimal *da* told me, "Narrate the story to Kishore Kumar".' The actor had delivered a few hit films at that time and Sen dutifully went to the singer-actor's house to check his interest.

Sen's narration of their first meeting for *Do Dooni Char* is a story that is typical of Kishore Kumar. 'I reached his place at the appointed time and sat in the hall, waiting. Suddenly, I saw that from behind a staircase, an eye was watching me. When our eyes met, he came out, laughing and saying, "You have seen me!" Then he took my hand and said, "OK, let's go and have breakfast." Saying which, he took me to his bedroom. I started the narration and, at that moment, an aeroplane flew overhead. He made a funny face and crawled under the bed. He then crawled out and said, "See my state! But tell Bimal *da* I loved the script."' Debu Sen adds that he heaved a sigh of relief.

The filming began. Sets were put up in Mohan Studio. Outdoor sequences were scheduled. The emotional attachment the unit felt to Bimal Roy Productions, and the need to keep the banner flying, urged them to suppress their emotions and keep the film going.

Tanuja was chosen to play the vivacious girlfriend while Sudha Rani, a fresh face from the Film and Television

Institute of India (FTII), was chosen to play wife to the married twin.

Bimal Roy's trust in Sen was justified. Debu Sen had proved his talent over the years.

Though he had moved to Calcutta from his home in Bihar because he wanted to play football, he ended up taking journalism instead. When he landed an offer in the Bombay office of Yugantar, he moved to the metropolis. Like his uncle, the well-known littérateur Jyotirmoy Roy, Sen wrote poetry in his spare time. His talent for comedy led to him being assigned to write some of the lighter scenes in Bimal Roy's films.

Sen's memories of shooting *Do Dooni Char* mostly revolve around the hero. According to him, Kishore Kumar sprung endless surprises and not all of them were pleasant.

Once, just around the lunch break at 1.30, the actor came up to Sen to say, 'Debu babu, *theek* time *hai*, I am hungry.' Sen coaxed him to give one last shot before breaking to eat. 'The shot had already been set up. I had the cameras rolling,' Debu remembers. 'It was a long shot of him coming down the street. But there was no sign of him. Then I get a phone call. He is calling from Bombay. He says, "Dada, I am here, I will return at 4 o'clock." And at four he would come.'

According to Tanuja, this was not an uncommon occurrence. Tanuja, who admits she was 'full of *josh*' at that time, points to working with Kishore Kumar as one of the highlights of the shooting stint. 'I loved working with him; we shared a tremendous relationship,' is how she describes the experience. In her fund of stories about the film is one where Kishore Kumar would whisper to her, '*Mai make-up karne nahin jaa raha hoon, mai ghar ja raha hoon. Kisi se mat bolna.*' The make-up room at Mohan Studio was a bit far away to one side and the star would escape, letting the unit wait for him to emerge. Tanuja explains that it was not irresponsible behaviour on his part. 'He had got a call telling him Madhubala was unwell and he just had to rush off. Of course, no one really knew that Madhubala was seriously ill; he would never let on. Everyone thought he was half-mad but he was deeply caring. Maybe he cared too much. Debu would go crazy, asking "where is he, where is he", to everyone. Of course, no one knew and I would also pretend and say, "He went for make-up."

Kishore Kumar would also entertain Tanuja with stories. 'He was a great storyteller. But,' the actress remembers, 'he would suddenly stop midway. "What happened?" I would ask, and he would say, "I don't know what is going to happen next – maybe I will know tomorrow – ". It was very irritating but he would laugh.'

Sen has his own fund of stories, including the fact that Kishore Kumar would tell him never to say 'hello' whenever he phoned. 'If you say hello, I will respond in a girl's voice,' the star used to say. But despite the eccentricities and truancy, Sen says that Kishore Kumar was a very lovable person and a deep friendship had developed between the two men.

Sen also could not understand why Kishore Kumar refused to watch the Bangla original. 'I told him to watch it, as this film was based on *Bhranti Bilash*, but he said, "No, no, Uttam is in it," as if that was explanation enough for his refusal.'

According to Tanuja, the role of the twin was perfectly suited to Kishore Kumar who was 'himself a multiple personality'. He would come to the set and ask, '*Aaj main koun hoon, shadi shuda ke nahin?*'

Kishore's presence was noticeable beyond the roles he played, as Tanuja remembers. He made special efforts to make his co-star comfortable. Perhaps it was Kishore Kumar who coined the phrase '*dedh* foot unit' to include Tanuja, her driver and her ayah. 'I am 5'2", my driver was 5'1" and my ayah was all of five feet." Despite the fact that she was only eighteen, with two or three films behind her including *Mem-Didi* (1961), *Hamari Yaad Aayegi* (1961) and *Benazir* (1964), and Kishore Kumar was not only a hit star after *Dilli Ka Thug* (1958) but also a singer of repute, he ensured his co-star was always at ease. 'I knew Hemant *da*, Bimal *da* and most of the people on the set thanks to my sister, Nutan, but I was still so much younger that I could easily feel left out. Kishore Kumar ensured I was not lonely or isolated.'

The love story angle of *Bhranti Bilash*, which hints at the sister-in-law being in love with her sister's husband, eluded the Hindi remake. Though Sen tried to explain the nuance to his actors, it was neither brought in nor magnified in the scenes between them.

Hemant Kumar, was, in Tanuja's words 'a gentleman, very quiet and refined', which echoes a common perception of the singer-composer. With a music composer at the helm, a few songs were almost mandatory. The Bangla version had included some songs, too, so there was a precedent. Krishna Kalle, Ranu Mukherjee (who as Hemant Kumar's daughter had inherited his ability to sing), Kishore Kumar and Manna Dey were signed on to sing the songs penned by Gulzar. 'In fact, we added two songs to accommodate Ranu,' Sen recalls.

'Once the shoot was completed – and it was done in less than forty days – we showed it to Bimal *da*. He watched the rushes carefully and said some changes needed to be made. He wanted a misunderstanding between the sisters and told me to add a few scenes. "Cut some other scenes if you need to fit this in," was his instruction, despite my telling him that the story was an adaptation of the Shakespearean play. So, I added a sequence where the sisters get annoyed with each other and a *Masterini* comes in and settles it.'

Sen also recollects the trouble that had come with shooting the double role and, more so, during the recording of the voice. 'Manik Chatterjee, third assistant, who later made *Ghar* (1978), was recording the sound and we had to physically move Kishore Kumar to "face" himself during the recordings,' he says.

Of the songs from *Do Dooni Char*, only one has survived and is counted as a perennial as it can be heard on the radio to date. Gulzar explains that he penned and visualized '*Hawaon pe likhdo hawaon ke naam*' as a song personifying the spirit of the film. 'Like "*Aankh micholi*", the game of hide and seek for children, the song has an illusive quality.' The presence of a child added an element of innocence to the song, which also showed in the character of the man singing it. The song was recorded in the hot springs of a natural jungle. Kishore Kumar passes by a girl carrying sticks on her head and the *aankh micholi* starts. Gulzar adds the nugget, that Debu told him 'much later' that the girl, whose mother had brought her to the shoot, that too accidentally, and who was quite unknown then, would later become well-known as Neetu Singh.

Gulzar also wrote a more rustic song, for a scene that was set in a fair, to allow Tanuja to spot the wrong Kishore Kumar and get the story rolling.

By the time *Do Dooni Char* was ready for the sound to be rerecorded, Bimal Roy had passed away. It was a sad and sombre unit that went through the motions, giving its best to the production.

The film was released; it ran for less than a week and vanished without a trace.

Sen believes the failure of the film was no one's fault, but due to an amalgamation of reasons. 'For one, there were flaws in the film. The United Producers had mixed ideas; each one of them would suggest a change here or there. Changes in scenes would kill the humour [and] subtle humour would be lost. Even loud humour suffered when sacrificed for the plot. No one had the time to listen to a full narration. They would listen to bits and pieces and demand additions or changes. Nuances were lost, the timing of the comedy went wrong because of the addition of scenes or lines, so I worked in bits. We could not appeal to Bimal *da* either, who could have set it right back on track, because the UP team was taking care of [both] him and the film's finances.' Not having Bimal *da* to support him was the biggest disappointment for the director.

'Then there was the fact that, except for a few lacklustre posters, there was absolutely no publicity for the film. No press shows, no ads in newspapers, nothing. The public was probably not even aware of its release in a few [of the] theatres in the city. Naturally, the halls were empty and the film was withdrawn.'

Gulzar says that he would have chosen a different cast; that known comedians like Kishore Kumar and Asit Sen were the wrong choice and someone more deadpan or unexpected would have added more punch to the story. 'Besides this, Debu, for whom this was a first venture, was working under a handicap. He would write out scenes, make small schedules and take it to Subodh *da*, who would use a red pencil and make small changes. This would continue in some manner even on locations. Again, we had to find cheap ways of making sets and use locations that would not strain the budget.'

All this control was detrimental to the flow of the film and seriously handicapped the director. Debu could not work on the film as he wanted, as constant changes were made to the scenes he planned.

The film's fate sealed Debu Sen's future as a director. He would make no more films; however, he wrote many. Among them was *Jeevan Sukh* (1983), which would be released only in Calcutta, and some Marathi and Gujarati cinema movies. Sen also went on to write twelve films for the Nepal film industry, doing it, as he said, 'for running the home'. He refused credit for his work. Also to his credit is the DD serial *Jagat Bandhu Ka Sansar*. Today, Sen is happy writing poetry, and the occasional prose, and keeps in touch with a few of his colleagues from those days. In turn, Sen is remembered with affection. When Gulzar was awarded the Dadasaheb Phalke Award, the poet sent a huge bouquet of flowers to Sen as 'it was Debu who took me to Bimal *da*.'

Post *Do Dooni Char*, Gulzar's career continued on an even keel with him writing both songs and scripts for Hrishikesh Mukherjee and other directors. He would also take on directing films. But deep in his mind, the story of two sets of twins and his favourite Shakespeare play, *A Comedy of Errors*, would lie waiting for a chance to surface again.

chapter six

The Comic Trail

Many Kinds of Laughter

ॐ

Though there is no doubt that Gulzar brought a new edge to comedy with *Do Dooni Char* and later, *Angoor*, much as the original writer of the story of identical twins had done, comedy had been an intrinsic part of Hindi cinema right from the early days of its inception.

As early as 1913, Dada Phalke, who is reported to have had a puckish sense of humour and a penchant for comedy, included in a film titled *Pithache Panje*, or *Hand Prints*, a scene where a woman gets wise to an amorous exchange between her husband and their house help. Borrowing from dramatic practice, Phalke often placed comic scenes between two dramatic scenes, even in his mythology-based works. Laughter was its own magnet and played its role in ensuring the audience appreciated the tense moments better.

Disguises, extended gags and attempts at ridicule marked much of the comedy in silent cinema. Despite the popularity and talent of some of the comedians, the comic film remained a 'side reel', ranging in duration from a single reel to ninety minutes, and none of the comic actors or directors of such films ever reached the level of a Chaplin or even a Laurel and Hardy in content, finesse or treatment. That Western comedies starring the fat and thin comedy duo was commonly shown on Indian cinema screens points to the fact that, with the advent of the talkies, Indian comedians found inspiration in their antics. In fact, comedians Nazir Ahmed Ghory and Manohar Janardhan Dixit (famously known as Ghory and Dixit) consciously created a Laurel and Hardy twosome, often seen in similar situations and clothes that were reminiscent of the originals, and the partnership endured many films. And to give them due credit, the two artists would put their soul into their performances and bring down the house.

Also claiming his place in the pantheon of comic actors was Noor Mohammad, who, after a film titled *Indian Charlie* (1933), renamed himself Charlie. How far the film, or his role in it, was a take-off of Chaplin is not clear, but the Indian Charlie acknowledged his inspiration and copied Chaplin's look down to the busy, mobile eyebrows and the toothbrush moustache. Slapstick combined with the resemblance kept Charlie going; and perhaps Charlie has to his credit the first vulgar comic scenes in Hindi cinema, in a film that was also directed by him. *Dhandhora* (1941) was predictably panned by critics but, as a portent of things to come, ran to a full house and became a huge hit.

Comedians continued to be part of mainstream cinema through the late forties; and well into the fifties, we saw comedian Gope, with his beaming face and portly figure, teaming up with the much thinner Yakub to recreate another Laurel and Hardy mystique.

Gope's name remains in the annals as the singer of the still popular song '*Mere piya gaye rangoon*', but it was Jeevan (perhaps more identifiable as Kiran Kumar's father) who added an edge to the comic persona. Jeevan, who would become almost synonymous with the divine messenger Narad, used his facial expressions and the rolling of his eyes to add a touch of comic to the acts of villainy he essayed on screen. Though Jeevan started his career as early as 1935, he continued to hold his own through three decades, starring with the likes of Dilip Kumar and Rajendra Kumar in hits like *Kohinoor* (1960) and *Kanoon* (1960). In *Kohinoor*, he was forced to let the hero have the upper hand, not only in the slap he receives on screen but also because the film proved the tragedy king's superior sense of comic timing. But we will come to that later.

Perhaps, like Pran, Jeevan endured because he created characteristics that made him identifiable and familiar in diverse roles. His nasal way of speaking was both a turn-off and a delight, causing audiences to settle back into their seats with relish at finding a familiar object to vent their hate on.

And one must not forget to mention Vinayak, the director, producer and comic genius who would give Hindi cinema its best loved *choti behen*, his daughter, the actress Nanda. Using satire as his medium and cloaking it in comedy, Vinayak found a way into his audience's hearts. His films resonated with their thoughts and the laughter he evoked took away the bite from the painful truths the films portrayed. Enough, then, to say that comedy reached a new sophistication with Master Vinayak; a far cry from its jerky, childlike beginnings. It was not long after this that the stage was set for a comedian who would bring much more to his roles than just humour.

Sanjit Narwekar, in his book *Eena Meena Deeka: The Story of Hindi Film Comedy*, gives perhaps the best delineation of the factors that made Kishore Kumar the unique actor he was:

His comic style was a combination of slapstick, visual gags, verbal word-play thrown in with a bit of romanticism. He was not a conventionally handsome man but he projected a kind of naive innocence, a vulnerability that went well with his image as a romantic hero. The fact that he could also sing added to the completeness of the screen image. Notice how all this blends together so seamlessly in a double role comedy like Debu Sen's *Do Dooni Char*, a reworking of Shakespeare's *A Comedy of Errors*, and note how much more fluidity Kishore Kumar imparts to the characters when compared to definitely a greater actor (also a terrific comedian) Sanjeev Kumar in Gulzar's *Angoor*, based on the same play.[5]

Narwekar goes on to add that Kishore Kumar's knowledge of music doubtless helped his sense of comic timing, which he demonstrated in film after film, including in classics like *Chalti Ka Naam Gaadi* (1958) and *Padosan* (1968).

Kishore Kumar benchmarked comedy, raising it to a stage where the hero could be comic without being vulgar or laughable. Indeed, his comic persona made him even more endearing and lovable, making the audience laugh with, rather than at, him.

Comedy had obviously come to stay by the early fifties. Directors and producers realized that comedy was not, as in the Greek and Roman times, less prestigious than tragedy. In fact, it was more of a challenge to script, produce and recreate on screen for audiences of diverse tastes spanning the entire spectrum of age and social class. Perhaps the most important film in this genre is *Albela* (1951). Starring a most

---

5   Sanjit Narwekar, *Eena Meena Deeka: The Story of Hindi Film Comedy*, New Delhi: Rupa and Co., 2005, p. 76.

unstarlike but nimble-footed Master Bhagwan as the hero opposite a magnetic Geeta Bali, the story of the unlikely dancing hero and the beautiful star, with its foot-tapping song and dance sequences and the undercurrent of comedy hiding the deeper pathos underlying the theme, was an unprecedented hit. Mingling emotions was an effective dramatic tool and could make for powerful situations.

Other filmmakers seemed to have discovered the same truth for themselves. So, when Guru Dutt and Bimal Roy took up their themes, often on social subjects, they still felt it necessary to add in codas that would help the audience take a breather. Unlike earlier such pauses, though, these directors were able to weld the persona of the comic-cum-character actor into the main narrative in such a way that their comedy not only evoked laughter but the character also took the story forward, sometimes in significant ways.

Johnny Walker's role in *Madhumati* (1958) as Dilip Kumar's man Friday and as the poet's friend in *Pyaasa* (1957) are two cases in point. These are also illustrative of how vital Johnny Walker's presence became in most films. The characteristic dialogue style, the facial expressions that were both identifiable and comical yet real and his ability to be the persona of the common man ensured that Badruddin Jamaluddin Kazi, the humble bus conductor who joined films as a comedian, stayed around to play comic cameos right through till the early 1970s in films like *Anand* (1971), where he aroused laughter against the backdrop of impending tragedy. More important was the fact that he carried Kishore Kumar's trend of being the comic singer forward. A film that did not have a song for Johnny was a rarity. And Rafi, the inimitable singer par excellence, even devised a special style for rendering the songs Johnny Walker would 'sing' on screen; that would bring a smile on the listeners' faces even when they were played on the radio.

Crowding the screen with efforts at evoking laughter were a host of other actors, each with their own signature style. Mukri, Dhumal, Jagdeep and, later, the eternal sidekick in all Joy Mukherjee romances, Rajendra Nath – all shone briefly, sometimes playing important character roles as they tickled the audience. Of Johar, who could move audiences to hysteria by delivering the funniest lines and going through hilarious situations with a deadpan face, all that can be said is that his talent as a comic was not given free rein. *Shagird* (1967), *Johar-Mehmood in Goa* (1965), *Bewaqoof* (1960) and *Chacha Zindabad* (1959) were some of the films where he showed his comic side before he moved into character roles and answering readers' queries in Filmfare with his tongue firmly in his cheek. But comedy took a new turn with another actor's coming of age who found his first foothold in films due to Johnny Walker.

Mehmood, like Johnny Walker, started his career in earnest with Guru Dutt Films, with *C.I.D.* (1956), where he was cast as the murderer. He played another negative character role as one of the hero's stepbrothers in *Pyaasa*.

Both won him some measure of attention. Till then, he had played a plethora of small roles that somehow belied his talent and left him unnoticed. Moving from strength to strength, as if his power to entertain the masses had finally been unleashed, Mehmood brought to Indian cinema comedy that spanned the entire spectrum; from the polished (*Pyar Kiye Jaa* [1966] and *Padosan*) to that bordering on the vulgar (*Gumnaam* [1965]). To quote S. Jhanvi in her series titled *No Laughing Matter* in the now extinct periodical *Lights Action Camera*:

> It is rumoured that many a leading man of that era was averse to being cast with him ... his smaller roles, too, are memorable for the creative insights he brought into them: the repetitive humming of '*La illahi*' in *Arzoo* (1969), '*O bhagatram ki behna*' in *Patthar Ke Sanam* and the Hyderabadi cook in *Gumnaam* who sings the cult favourite '*Hum kale hain to kya hua*'. Like Walker, he stole scenes from the biggest stars and had audiences demanding and expecting him to have songs of his own to sing. Mehmood was perhaps the first and the last comedian to hold a film on his own strength. In *Bombay to Goa* (1972), Amitabh, yet to find his stardom, plays second fiddle to him! With hit co-star pairings, first with Shobha Khote and later with Aruna Irani, he could bring in romantic shades to his roles. And when he teamed with Amitabh or

Johar, both of whom had a definite flair for comedy (and coincidentally, both films were set against a Goa theme), the result was pure fun.

Mehmood's most lasting contribution to cinema must surely be through the films he made. Combining his image as a comedian and an on-screen singer, Mehmood acted in movies like *Chhote Nawab* (1961), *Bhoot Bungla* (1965) which he also wrote and directed, *Padosan*, *Sabse Bada Rupaiya* (1976) and *Kunwara Baap* (1974). The latter two films had social themes, which somehow took away from the image of the star, but his other major contribution was the fact that all his films had good music with new music directors wielding the baton effectively. It was a step that would take comedy in Indian cinema to the next level, with songs supplementing the comic scenes.

But by the late seventies, the entire mood was turning; the Angry Young Man had arrived. And as he grew in stature with every film, Amitabh Bachchan's very presence crowded out most of his co-stars. When directors discovered his sense of timing, the fate of the sidekick comedian was sealed.

Comedy itself had fallen in bad times. Double meaning dialogues, slapstick routines and downright vulgarity had the masses in thrall, taking the comic act to a degrading low. Even though Govinda took on the mantle that actors like Dilip Kumar had worn in the past, playing the hero with comic ease, the sophistication was missing. Comedy was back in the pits. No wonder that songs like '*My name is Anthony Gonsalves*', where Bachchan shows off his comic side with both smooth sophistication and perfect timing, became to audiences what '*Sar jo tera chakraye*' had been in earlier decades: hummable, laughable fun. Only, the persona of the comic was now a facet of the hero.

Only a quiet phalanx of directors kept the flame of humour burning. They seem to have taken a leaf straight out of Bharata Muni's Natya Shastra in their approach to comedy.

In the section that deals with the nine rasas and their use in theatre, the Natya Shastra expounds on comedy and divides it into many types. One of them is the Prakarana, or a lengthy comedy that spans five to ten acts.

Prakarana, roughly corresponds with Aristotelian comedy. These plays are about middle-class characters invented by the playwright. The stories take place outside of palaces and royal circles, in the lanes and houses of the town, and are concerned with middle-class interests in money, love, legal justice and bourgeois honour. With plots hanging on the complications of mistaken identities, petty revenge, theft and political intrigue, Prakarana plays also end happily. At least, like Natakas, Prakaranas affirm the identities of their middle-class heroes and their place in the permanent cosmic order. Shudraka's *Mrcchakatika* (The Little Clay Cart) is the best-known example of a Prakarana.

Hrishikesh Mukherjee, Basu Chatterjee and Sai Paranjpye mined the middle class for their insecurities, their preoccupations with small triumphs and setbacks, their value systems and social mores to create a genre that had the audience sit up and notice. Themes ranged from household politics (*Bawarchi* [1972] and *Khubsoorat* [1980] by Hrishikesh Mukherjee; *Khatta Meetha* [1978] and *Piya Ka Ghar* [1972] by Basu Chatterjee) to love triangles (Chatterjee's *Chhoti Si Baat* [1976] and Sai's *Katha* [1983]) to more serious issues of social and political relevance (as in Sai's *Jaane Bhi Do Yaaro* [1983]). Using dialogue, situations and disguise to great effect, the movies were complete entertainers and dispelled the angst that the upward surging middle class was experiencing at that time. The films also created space for the real-life hero. Not a swashbuckling, one-man wonder who could do no wrong but a more identifiable common man who laughed at himself and bumbled his way to a happy ending. Amol Palekar, Utpal Dutt, A.K. Hangal, Dinesh Thakur, Ravi Baswani, Deven Verma and, among the women, Bindiya Goswami, Dina Pathak and Deepti Naval were among those who shone in roles that they played perfectly to bring in humour that rang true.

Surprise performances by well-established stars like Rajesh Khanna in *Anand* and *Bawarchi*, Rekha and Ashok Kumar in *Khubsoorat*, Om Prakash, Jaya Bhaduri, Sharmila Tagore and Amitabh Bachchan proved that when required, with the right script and director, most of Hindi cinema's stars could rise to delivering humour effectively.

If Amol Palekar, Utpal Dutt and Dina Pathak were the most enduring stars of this new genre, another important contributor was the dialogue and screenplay writer. Gulzar admits that his work with Hrishikesh Mukherjee gave him the springboard to write and direct his own comedy, *Angoor*.

Honing his inherent skills in timing and writing catchy turns of phrases that could evoke laughter with their element of surprise, Gulzar would find himself well-prepared when the time came to direct his first comedy. He would also by then have a clear understanding of how to choose his actors and pitch them against each other, so they worked as perfect foils and catalysts, to bring out their very different sparkle. But before we stop to examine and smile over Gulzar's unique brand of comedy, let us continue down the road of comedy and venture into the 1990s, where sharp dips and turns took comedy to a level never seen before.

Almost as if the wave of sophisticated comedy evidenced not just in mainstream films by Basu Chatterjee and Hrishikesh Mukherjee but also in films like *Jaane Bhi Do Yaaro* and *Katha* had never existed, comedy took a slide that brought it to a sudden, unexpected low.

Aiming their double meaning dialogues at the lowest denominator in the audience, actors like the otherwise hugely talented Kader Khan (who had been part of the team writing memorable dialogues for *Mughal-e-Azam* [1960] and wrote *Khel Khel Mein* [1975]) and Shakti Kapoor ensured that ribald, back slapping humour raged in theatre halls for almost a decade. Adding star power to their presence was 'the boy next door', the nimble-footed, pleasant-faced Govinda. With David Dhawan, who had discovered his funny bone and immense mass appeal, Govinda would go on to deliver a series of almost unstoppable hits.

But films like *Hera Pheri* (2000), *Hum Tum* (2004) and the Munnabhai series tilted the scales again, bringing comedy to a more acceptable level and using it as much to deliver a lesson as to raise laughter.

Today, comedy seems to be waiting for a new avatar. The Salman brand of comedy holds its followers in thrall and flashes of humour are glimpsed in films like *Piku* (2015) and *PK* (2014). But the world of cinema is waiting for the likes of Basu Chatterjee and Hrishikesh Mukherjee to take centre stage once more and give cinegoers a taste of clean, honest fun.

chapter seven

The Long Road to *Angoor*

ജ

The story of how Gulzar started working in films is well-known enough to not need repeating here; yet it is a story so sweet in its element of serendipity that it merits at least a brief retelling.

So it happened that musician S.D. Burman, who was music director for Bimal Roy's recreation of the *Devdas* (1936) saga written by Sarat Chandra Chatterjee, fell out with the lyricist for the film, Shailendra, and refused to work with him in a fit of pique. A substitute song writer had to be found urgently as a song picturization was next on the schedule and any delay would mean financial and time setbacks.

Generous as he was of spirit, Shailendra mentioned to Bimal *da*'s assistant Debu Sen that he knew a young poet who could perhaps deliver at a short notice; that said poet was currently making ends meet by working as a touch-up painter at a garage but might be amenable to the idea. When approached, the story goes, Gulzar was unwilling to delve into the world of films; his mission being to establish himself as a poet in literary circles. But Sen, and the fact that Bimal Roy Productions was in dire straits for want of a song writer, persuaded him to put his skills to good use. History notes that Gulzar's first song '*Mora gora ang laile*' for the film *Bandini* (1963) was an intimation of the fount of lyrics that were to follow over the years and that its imagery added its weight to the film's visual poetry. Bimal Roy, impressed by the young poet's talent, asked him to continue with his unit.

'I was taken on as assistant to the director on *Kabuliwala*,' Gulzar recollects. 'The film was being written by S. Khalil, who had directed *Benazir* in 1964 under Bimal Roy's banner. Khalil was a wonderful person, a paan addict like S.D. Burman, with whom he had collaborated in *Benazir*, for which Burman *da* had made music.' Besides assisting Khalil, Gulzar was also pressed into service as song writer for *Kabuliwala* and wrote four out of the five songs in the film. The still popular patriotic '*Ay mere pyaare watan*' was written by Prem Dhawan.

Based on a short story by Rabindranath Tagore, the film was directed by Hemen Gupta, with Salil Choudhury scoring the music. Gulzar wrote '*Ganga aaye kahan se*', sung by Hemant Kumar, '*O ya qurban*', sung by Mohammed Rafi, and the title song, '*Kabuliwala*', which Hemant Kumar sang with Usha Mangeshkar.

During the writing of the screenplay, Gulzar realized that 'some scenes would not work for me. I would say, "There is too much dialogue; let us cut it down."' He adds self-deprecatingly, 'When we know little, we imagine we know so much, so we speak up, sometimes out of turn. But that is what I did.

'Most of the discussions would be with everyone concerned present and that included Bimal *da*, who would be reclining on a chair. He was a man of few words; he would think for a moment and say "hmmm". That "hmmm" was very eloquent. It had so many meanings and we learnt to understand and interpret them correctly as we worked with him. Then, he would turn to me and say, "You write," and Khalil would nod and say, "Yes, yes, you write." He was also very encouraging and would say, "Give us a new version. Let us see."'

Gulzar was soon writing scenes as well as songs.

Gulzar remembers that *Bandini* had been completed and *Prem Patra*'s schedule was coming to an end. But Rajinder Krishan, the lyricist, was very busy, holding up the shooting and upsetting Bimal *da*, who was directing the film. 'When Rajinder ji finally delivered the song, Bimal *da* was not happy with it and asked me to write the song. "If I don't give your name, is it okay?" he asked. I said [that] yes, it was fine.' Gulzar wrote '*Saawan ki raaton mein*' and it was to go under Rajinder Krishan's name, but luck decreed otherwise. 'HMV was on strike at that time and by the time the record came out, someone had included my name in the credits,' Gulzar says, laughing.

He recounts how he got to write the script for an entire film. When *Do Dooni Char* was launched, the original script was in Bangla. 'Nabendu[6] had written the script and Paul had translated it into Hindi but Bimal *da* was not quite happy with the result. Perhaps knowing my background in literature, he turned to me and said, "Gulzar, you try." Sen, who was directing, concurred.'

Gulzar's experience with Bimal Roy Productions was fruitful in that he watched and learnt from the master himself, honing his skills in many departments of filmmaking.

It was Hemant Kumar, 'a tall man with a taller heart', who would give Gulzar the next boost. 'He helped everyone from the unit to find other anchors when Bimal Roy Productions started disintegrating.' Gulzar soon found work as the dialogue and song writer for Hrishikesh Mukherjee's film, *Aashirwad* (1968). 'Hemant *da* put me in touch with Hrishi *da* and it was the start of a very productive period,' according to Gulzar. Two years later, he would script *Anand*, the story of a 'never say die' man in the terminal

6   Nabendu Ghosh was a writer who worked with Bimal Roy and considered him his guru. He wrote the screenplays of, among others, *Parineeta*, *Yahudi*, *Devdas*, *Sujata* and *Bandini*.

phase of cancer. The film would give Gulzar the status as a scriptwriter of no mean talent. It was also his first real foray into humour that revolved on both words and comic characters. Though the failure of *Do Dooni Char* devastated Debu Sen, who retreated to writing in Bangla, Gulzar did not give up. He also nursed an idea of getting into direction. 'I wanted to become a director. I felt I was stuck in writing. Hemant *da* promised me a break,' he remembers. 'He said, "*Faraar ke baad* ..." but it did not happen; he could not make another film just then. I wanted to make a patriotic film. Then I wanted to make *Do Dooni Char* again. But everyone said, "Why make a flop film again?"'

Putting the idea of the comedy on the back burner, Gulzar busied himself with other projects. He wrote the script for the remake of Tapan Sinha's Bangla hit, *Apanjan* (1968), but the film did not get made in Hindi; Gulzar would later direct it as *Mere Apne* (1971). 'By the time I had done *Sunghursh* (1968), *Anand* and *Khamoshi* (1970), I was confident enough to move away from *Apanjan* and make *Mere Apne* differently. While the original Bangla film had lavish dream sequences, the Hindi version was close to the ground. Tapan Sinha had made a Hindi film in Bengali; I made a Bengali film in Hindi! I started doing work in earnest, doing other films, but *Do Dooni Char* kept reappearing. It just would not go away.'

Gulzar pressed his case when Yash Johar, who was then working with Rakhi, approached him to make a film for him. 'Once again, I brought up the subject. I said, "Let's make a comedy." "Which one?" Johar asked. "*Do Dooni Char*," I promptly replied.' Yash Johar made the necessary enquiries, trying to gauge what the response to the film would be. 'He came back to me and hit his hand on his head. "It was a four-day flop," he said, vehemently countering all my arguments in the film's favour. So I offered him *Ijaazat* (1987), based on a short story. He shook his head again. "I don't think you can survive in this industry," he said. "You are a gone case. Rakhiji requested me to meet you, so I did, but I can't look after you. How can you make a film with a married woman as your heroine?"'

If Gulzar was dejected with the repeated rejection of his idea of remaking the comedy, he does not mention it. 'I waited' is how he succinctly puts it.

chapter eight

An Affair with Shakespeare

ɕ

Gulzar first met Shakespeare 'when he was part of my college syllabus, which has not changed since British times. Kalidas is still waiting his turn.'

Gulzar read *Twelfth Night* in school and can quote the passage 'if music be the food of love, play on …' as one of the passages still familiar to him. In college, he delved deeper into the Bard's works. He read *Romeo and Juliet* as well as *A Comedy of Errors*, even though these were not in his course. *Julius Caesar* was part of the syllabus, so he read that too. By then, 'Shakespeare was a familiar person whom I enjoyed always. I was in awe of his writing; he was a great writer. Even in school, though we spoke less in English, we would copy the way the teachers recited from his texts. This is something you imbibe easily in school years.' After college too, Gulzar's connection with the playwright continued. He read *Othello* and *Macbeth* and marvelled at their structure. 'The great thing about him is how he makes the plot so interesting … *ek se ek* … the intricacies were the fascinating part. Like the "Ides of March", a phrase thrown casually by a cobbler in the street that becomes meaningful much later.'

Another aspect that fascinated the aspiring writer in Gulzar was that he could look at the Bard's texts like pure writing. 'Unlike the Ramayana or the Mahabharata or even the Odyssey, one can be friendly with them, even wink at his work. And he was a craftsman whose craft influenced so many, in languages beyond his knowledge: Urdu, Bangla, Hindi, Punjabi.'

Gulzar himself honed his writing skills by reading all the languages he could. 'The influence comes in,' he believes. Adding to these were what his associations with diverse writers and thinkers like Salil Choudhury, Ali Sardar Jafri, Chekhov, Tolstoy, the Progressive Writers' Association (PWA), Habib Tanvir and Sahir Ludhianvi brought to his thinking and expression as influencers. Over the years of his reading, the 'classics retreated and social issues became more relevant; one started participating in them. The romanticism of Balzac, Zola and Maupassant gave way to Ghalib, Tagore. *My Glorious Brothers*, *Spartacus* and *The Naked God* were strong influences. When I came to work with Bimal Roy, I came into the flow of the company of leftists like Shailendra and those making films like *Do Bigha Zamin* (1953).'

Yet, when asked to write a comedy based on *A Comedy of Errors*, Gulzar was delighted to accept it. In fact, the story somehow stayed alive in his subconscious, urging him to take a chance at converting it to film again. 'I kept hoping someone would think like I did and find the comedy worth making,' Gulzar recounts. 'And, sure enough, Shakespeare came back to me. It was full circle.' Gulzar met a Mr Jai Singh, who was visiting Bombay from Moradabad in UP. Gulzar remembers that he was the chairman of a bank and active in politics. 'Everyone called him Babuji. I can still hear him; he had a high pitched voice … but he also had a big heart. I told him the history of *Do Dooni Char* and added that the script of the film was still with me. It was a sound script; the movie, I explained, had failed for other reasons beyond our control. His first reaction was, "Do it." He said, "I read the play in college and loved it. Such a funny play." And so, he was ready. The project was on!'

Though a large-hearted, jovial and simple person from a small town, 'Babuji was very money savvy. He wanted me to narrate the script. I narrated it to him. At every turn, he would anticipate the situation. He laughed heartily and his son-in-law, Rajinder Singh, would join in. It was such an enjoyable time, with much laughter and sharing. It was childlike fun.'

When it came to finding a name for the film, Gulzar suggested *Angoor* because he wanted something very unusual. 'Babuji quickly said, "It will be sour grapes for all of them who said no to the idea of making the film!" I told him I will justify the title. Of course, the name mystified most people. They would say, "But *angoor* is a fruit, na?"'

But Gulzar did not worry over this. His dream was about to come to fruition. Now, his challenge was to make a film that would not suffer the same fate as *Do Dooni Char*.

chapter nine

Angoor

A Sweet Sour Story

ॐ

According to the nomenclature given to such plays in the Natya Shastra, *Angoor*, as well as its two predecessors, are Vyayoga plays given that the action of the comedy is contained within the time frame of a single day.

Gulzar continued with the structure that had been outlined first in *Bhranti Bilash* and then in *Do Dooni Char*, adding changes to suit the more modern audience. The Indian versions all deviated from Shakespeare's original in some marked respects. Gulzar did away with the background story of the enmity between cities and the punishment that would be given to a visitor from the rival city as such a theme would not be relevant in the modern Indian context. Divesting the story of the period trappings, and concentrating on just the two sets of twins and their presence in the same town, gave enough scope for humour through dialogue and comic situations.

The story starts by establishing how the unnatural happening of two sets of twins with each pair carrying an identical name came about. Raj Tilak, played in his inimitable style by Utpal Dutt, and his wife, an unnamed woman played by Shammi, are preparing to travel by sea. This is established by means of a joke, where the wife explains why she is a bit nervous of the journey ahead because she cannot swim and thus would have preferred to fly (which would not do for our story at all, as survivors of a plane crash are rare compared to those of a shipwreck). The husband retorts that he is as wary of flying as he has never learnt to fly. It might be an old joke but it helps establish why, in modern times, this well-off couple is taking the sea route rather than the aeroplane. Also established is the confusion that the identical twin boys are causing their parents and the quick explanation as to why the father has named them both Ashok. 'When they grow up a bit and we are able to tell them apart better, we will give them separate names,' he says. The same principle is applied to the twin babies they adopt after they are found abandoned inside a temple. Because they somewhat resemble the Nepalese, these twins are named Bahadur. Of course, by the time Deven Verma comes on the scene, the reason for the name is forgotten and the name Bahadur establishes the fact that Deven plays servant to Sanjeev Kumar in both roles.

The grown-up twins are introduced differently. One is a prosperous, married man, in the process of being seduced by his wife. The other is a lover of detective stories, who is on his way to somewhere in a first-class compartment, which seems full of dark potential.

Right from the very beginning, it is evident that the marriage between Ashok 1 and Sudha rides on stormy waters. Being insecure, demanding and suspicious by nature, the wife, despite her obvious physical charms, is capable of driving her more sensible husband to the edge. Her repeated demands for a costly necklace, expressed in a seductive bedroom song and followed up with jibes and taunts over breakfast, gets the story rolling. Ashok 1 storms out of the house, vowing not to return sans the aforementioned coveted bauble. During the unpleasant breakfast exchange, we also hear of 'the other woman', Alka. Later, this will prove a red herring.

Even as Ashok 1 leaves the scene, Ashok 2 enters; quite a different kettle of fish, though he looks as if he belongs to the same pond. Armed with a murder mystery book, one lakh rupees and Bahadur 2 accompanying him to play Jeeves to his every want, Ashok 2 is on his way to where his twin resides, though he does not know it. He lives a night's journey by train away with his mother, Mrs Raj Tilak. Thoroughly psyched by the book he is reading and by the strangely familiar way the ticket collector addresses him, Ashok 2 decides that a gang has come to know that he is carrying cash and that he must hide it, setting out decoys to thwart any attempt at separating him from his booty. Thus, a second line of potential for humour is established.

The plot gets thicker. Ashok 1 checks on the necklace, which seems to take forever getting made. It is promised to him by nine that night, which means that he must hang around without going home till then. Meanwhile, Ashok 2 has found a hotel where he needs must pretend he is not staying to decoy the inquisitive small-town taxi driver who ferries him there. He hides the money in the cupboard, sets Bahadur to guard it with the zealousness of a snake guarding treasure and gives him a code that he will use to ensure the door is opened only for him when he returns. Bahadur, who we know likes his bhang, is told to strictly stay off the substance.

Despite his fears of ambush and attack, Ashok 2 manages a satisfactory visit to the property he has come to inspect and takes a bus back to the town. His sanguineness is shattered when he sees Bahadur buying vegetables at a market close to the bus stop. Upset at the obvious disobedience of his command that Bahadur should not even open the door, he accosts the servant, only to enter a labyrinth of dialogues that leave him confused, angry and disturbed. Convinced that Bahadur has had a generous helping of bhang, he rushes to his room to find his servant dutifully opening the door on hearing the code song.

Meanwhile, Bahadur 1, who had been buying vegetables at Sudha's command, rushes home with the juicy story that his master has gone mad in his anger. We meet here, once again, the placatory sister-in-law, Tanu, who is also convinced that something is wrong. Even as Sudha dissolves into tears over her husband's lost mind, Tanu sends Bahadur to fetch him home. Tanu, we are told, has a musical performance that evening and her family needs to attend it too!

Bahadur 1 cannot locate Ashok because he looks for him at Alka's place and is advised to seek him out at the jewellers'. No one thinks of looking for him in the office, which is the logical place he should be. It is the jeweller, Chedilal, who suggests that Ashok could be in his office as the necklace would not be ready till nine in the evening. Ashok is whiling away the hours in his office. His anger has made him blank out everything except his need to deliver the necklace and shut his wife's taunts for the moment at least; he predictably gives Tanu's show a miss. But with time to kill, the other set of twins reach the hall. Tanu notices and sends the manager to escort them to the reserved seats in the front row.

Much confusion follows over expectations and perceived behavioural shifts. After an altercation where everyone speaks at cross-purposes, Ashok 2 is carried home to safety. Bahadur 2 follows.

Scenes now tumble one after another at a fast pace. Bahadur is held in the kitchen by his 'wife', Prema, who sets him to work. Equally triumphantly, Sudha holds her 'husband' prisoner, plying him with drinks. It is up to Bahadur to think up an escape plan and he puts his bhang to effective use, mixing it with the pakoras and ensuring the women have plenty of it.

Ashok 1 fares no better. The necklace is still not ready; Mansoor Mia, the hefty craftsman setting, polishing and finishing the necklace, needs more time. Ashok 1 cannot go home but when he does give in to Bahadur's insistence, he finds himself unable to enter. The door stays stubbornly shut, kept that way, he believes, by a stubborn wife; worse still, he is greeted by the threatening barks of a dog he does not own from within the house. There is a gentle irony in the fact that he is indirectly driven by his wife's actions to her 'rival' Alka's place, where he decides to stay for the night.

Seeing the entire household in the grip of bhang or liquor, Bahadur 2 also succumbs to the lure and eats the spiked pakoras, drifting into sleep soon after. However, his habit of taking bhang makes him wake up easily enough with his wits about him. His code song summons the master downstairs and, after a lucky break in which the key to the main door is procured from inside Prema's blouse, the two decide to run away from the enchanted city and repair for home.

Bahadur is dispatched to get train tickets while Ashok waits in an auto to go to Imperial Hotel. This is when Mansoor Mia, carrying the necklace as promised, spots him and leaves the box with Ashok despite remonstrations. Naturally there is high drama when the right Ashok reaches the jeweller to claim his long-delayed necklace and, with one thing and another, the entire lot reaches the police station. The station-in-charge is a friend but he must do his duty. He asks for five thousand rupees as surety to allow Ashok 1 to go home and sort things out.

More confusion ensues. Wrong servants meet right masters and finally all the dramatis personae reach the police station where the combinations are matched and all ends well.

The movie ends with the lost son and the daughter-in-law being reunited with the mother and the hint of another daughter-in-law in the air. We are not shown what transpired in the closed room between an alcohol-soaked Ashok 2 and Tanu, but she does talk of a kiss and there is this loose thread that will tie nicely if the twin brother should wed the sister-in-law. One believes that when that happens, Ashok 1 will be happy to have Tanu around to keep his wife rooted in reality.

Maybe there is scope for another rollicking comedy there, a sequel maybe.

chapter ten

A Set of Crafty Characters

☙

Angoor has seven main characters. Besides this, there are also supporting characters who add to the comic element through dialogues and action.

The main challenge for Gulzar as a writer and director was to find a way of creating two sets of twins who looked and dressed similarly enough to confuse the other characters, but yet were clearly demarcated in the minds of the audience. Gulzar took recourse to 'simple visual hints to separate their identities and help the audience know which one is on-screen'.

Ashok

Of course, there are two Ashoks and the differences between them are quite marked. One is married. Let us call him Ashok 1.

Ashok 1

Maybe there was a subconscious message in the fact that Ashok 1 wears his spotless white kurta buttoned up all the way to his neck. He is, after all, an upright and respectable married man; a fact that is underlined by the jeweller who is ready to hand over a costly diamond- and ruby-encrusted gold necklace to him before receiving payment, or even an advance, for the same.

As the story progresses, Ashok 1's personality becomes clearer, along with his foibles and hates. He takes snuff, gets angry easily and there is a feudal streak in him, evidenced by the fact that he thinks nothing of raising his hand against Bahadur with whom he has actually grown up almost fraternally. He likes to drink and thus causes his wife some concern. He likes his food spicy. He flaunts a superior attitude towards his wife, bordering on chauvinism, and he is stingy. Bahadur bears witness to this fact when he says that all he has ever received from his master in cash has been ten rupees and there is only a promise of accounts being brought up to date but no sign of the money due to him as wages. And, though it has no impact on the story, he hates dogs.

Ashok 2

In contrast to his twin, Ashok 2 is more genial and less urbane. Sanjeev Kumar brings this about very subtly in ways that are not evident but yet communicate this difference. It is in the carriage of the torso, in the walk, in his way of looking around or addressing people.

Gulzar adds: 'Sanjeev Kumar's contribution was tremendous. I had written simply, "I know you are part of a gang." But the way he said the word gang, "gaang", added so much.'

To show his more easygoing nature, perhaps, Ashok 2's kurta is left unbuttoned at the neck. The difference is not immediately noticeable; it is as if Gulzar is playing a secret game of spot the differences with the audience. Ashok 2 is, of course, unmarried, loves detective stories and thrillers and is childlike enough to get involved in them while reading and carry the feeling of threat into his own life. It makes him suspicious by nature where his safety and that of the considerable sum (in those days) of one lakh rupees he is carrying is concerned. Though he is close enough to be a brother to Bahadur, he slaps him when he thinks Bahadur has been careless or is on dope. (In fact, Ashok 2 slaps Bahadur 1 in the bazaar, thinking he is 2 and under the influence of bhang.) His simplicity can come across as simpleminded thickheadedness, as in the scene when he is told that Bahadur is going to be a father and he questions his Bahadur repeatedly about it. He is also, unlike most Hindi film heroes who are musically blessed, completely unable to carry a tune. And unlike his twin, who loves *baingan*s (eggplant), he hates the vegetable.

It is worth a thought to consider whether the differences between the twins were consciously created by Gulzar to show that one was brought up by the father, and was thus more macho, self-assured and conscious of his worldly station, while the other, being a mother's boy, was gentler, less self-assured and more given to the dreamier side of life.

Bahadur

The same principles come into play here to help the audience differentiate between the Bahadur twins. To Deven Verma's credit, he plays the roles so deftly, enunciating in subtle ways the differences between the two, that both come across as distinct personalities. Little wonder he won the Filmfare award for his role(s).

Bahadur 1

Bahadur 1 is Ashok 1's servant. Like his twin, he wears long sleeved kurtas but, unlike him, he rolls up the sleeves. This helps us identify him more easily. He also wears an iron *kara* on one hand and calls our attention to it by swearing upon it at one point in the film. Bahadur 1 is married to a wife who dotes on him, mothers him and has recruited him to help her in the kitchen. So, we see Bahadur 1 mixing the dough for rotis, washing vessels, or at least agreeing to do so, since Gulzar spares us the mundanities of such visuals. Bahadur 1 is appropriately servile to an extent to Ashok 1; his manner, like that of a servant towards his master. In an urban, well-off household as the one Ashok 1 has grown up in, the class difference is easy to maintain. It also makes him vulnerable by nature. He cries easily and feels sympathy for Moushumi, Ashok's wife, who he thinks is treated in a cavalier manner by Ashok 1.

Bahadur 2

Perhaps implying the fact that Bahadur 2, brought up by Ashok's mother, has had privileges and affection that his twin might not have enjoyed in a male dominated household, Bahadur 2 enjoys a more genial relationship with his master. It is much more informal and relaxed. More often than not, he is the one who steers his master when he wanders off from the real world into the one his reading of thrillers creates for him. Bahadur 2 is logical and more in control of situations. Yet his bond with Ashok 2 is so strong that he buys into the gang story and, when matters become really confusing, begins to believe it to be true. In the scene where he eats the bhang-soaked pakoras by himself, his expressions and body language is a master stroke of acting by Deven Verma and one of the best scenes in Hindi comedy. And yes, Bahadur 2 can carry a tune, even when the bhang gets the better of him!

Sudha

In her character we have the typical 1970s unlettered, pampered, upper middle-class woman. She is well-groomed, dresses impeccably at all times and wears make-up. She is aware of her charms but depends completely on them alone to get her way and hold her man, which is why she gets completely insecure if he even looks at another woman. Sudha is temperamental and almost hysterical at times. She can be weak and silly, and sensual and sexual, depending on the circumstance her limited exposure to life has given her. She is, of course, fond of jewellery and imagines that getting a necklace from her husband is proof of his love for her; a fact that is brought out beautifully in a song – *yaad to hogi kuch bhuli bisari aise barsi thi chand si misari*.

Completely illogical and prone to tears at the slightest provocation, Gulzar's heroine is his way of highlighting the manipulative side of women who depend on their men for emotional and financial sustenance. And yes, she will stoop to cheating at cards, because she has to have the upper hand somewhere!

Prema

Aruna Irani brings to Prema a softness that is not often a part of the roles given to her. Prema is efficient, gentle yet matter-of-fact and very comfortable with her role in Ashok 1's household. She loves her husband a lot but is not above bossing him around, even as she worries about his well-being. Almost as a foil to the rest of the cast, Prema is not comic. She is one of the pillars around which the story winds and she is the perfect foil to Deven Verma as both Bahadurs.

Tanu

In an oblique, asexual way, Tanu makes the bawdy line that says the *saali* is '*adhi gharwali*' ring true. Though there is no hint of an incestuous interest on either side, her presence as the grounded, unemotional, balanced younger sister of the heroine makes her take charge of the household. So, it is to her that everyone turns to in moments of crisis and it is in her hands that the keys to the almirahs repose; when Bahadur 1 needs five thousand rupees as surety at the police station, it is to Tanu he addresses the note and the request, knowing that addressing it to his wife will only result in tears, questions and panic.

Tanu sings. Gulzar admits he was forced to put in the song and did it as naturally as it could be done and, like his guru, Bimal Roy, he managed to use the song to take the story forward. Also, in small mannerisms, Gulzar ensured that Tanu emerged as a person in her own right. The dress, so different from her immaculate wifely sister, the large glasses that Deepti Naval 'had to learn with much difficulty how to push up my nose with a sniff and which I realize I did not get as perfectly as Gulzar sahib wanted it,' all added to her no-nonsense, younger, caring sister persona. It is only in the last scene, when Tanu is half-dreamy and recounting the kiss she received from Ashok 2, that we notice a hint of unspoken dreams of romance. Otherwise, Tanu is the rock on which the story rests when the confusion gets confounding.

Of the supporting cast, only Mansoor Mia, the jewellery craftsman, and Ganeshilal, the precious stone polisher, have roles that add to the comedy quotient.

Mansoor Mia

Typically a man of the world, he works on fine jewellery that he knows from experience are baubles men use to seduce women. His cynicism makes him suspect that the necklace Ashok has ordered is indeed for his wife. More so, when Ashok acts, he believes, strangely, refusing to accept the necklace and even the fact that he is married. Mansoor is tough-looking but speaks in poetic Urdu, Gulzar's own favoured language, and the combination of home truths with the flowery terminology is perfect for Ashok's reactions to bounce off from. Mansoor Mia was Gulzar's way of ensuring his film drew laughter from all sections of the audience and, in the process, gave rein to his own love of Urdu.

Ganeshilal

Ganeshilal is typical of those who ply crafts that depend on others to find clientele. He cuts, facets and polishes diamonds and other precious stones. Though his craft is vital to making the perfect ornament, he is dependent upon the jeweller, who will not pay him till he himself is paid for the final product. This has made Ganeshilal into a strange mix of aggressive and servile. He wheedles his way through business deals, has a strong code that will not mix friendship with work and tries to pin down payment modes and times, as otherwise he knows the delays in the delivery of an ornament and the release of payment for the same will, in turn, leave him hanging too. His humour irritates, as he continues to insist on his deadline, and there is a strange satisfaction when the police inspector tells him to shut up. But, like a snake in a basket, he rears once in a while to put in his choral demand for what is actually his due. Combined with Mansoor Mia and the jeweller Chedilal, Ganeshilal creates the third angle of a scene where their distinct personalities set off one another to comic advantage.

Alka

Alka is probably the only weakly sketched character in this epoch-making comedy. She wears saffron and a *rudraksha* necklace to indicate to the audience that there is only a platonic relationship between her and Ashok 1, despite Sudha's suspicions. She is down to earth, caring up to a point and her effort at ensuring Ashok 1 has breakfast before leaving for office is to place an entire loaf of bread, a cake and fruits on the table and tell him to eat well before leaving. Her patience in the face of Sudha's accusations that the necklace was made for her, and she should keep it, only serves to highlight Sudha's irrational thinking. Alka herself does not stand out as a complete person but is more of a prop to help move the story forward.

chapter eleven

The Gulzar–Pancham Brand of Music

ॐ

Three songs punctuate the story of *Angoor*, commas that Shakespeare or his audience might never have expected in an adaptation of the original. But Indian audiences are conditioned to want song and dance sequences in cinema, which is viewed mainly as a venue that provides an escape from the tribulations of daily life, and so would not deign to watch a film without songs. Thus, right from *Bhranti Bilash,* the adaptation of *A Comedy of Errors* included songs. Of course, Debu Sen's film's songs were a corollary of the fact that music director Hemant Kumar was part of United Producers. Gulzar wrote those numbers too. When it came to *Angoor*, Gulzar, now turned director, decided the songs would have to be more in keeping with changed times. The situations would, therefore, be changed accordingly.

Unlike in *Do Dooni Char*, where two of the songs are filmed between the sisters with Tanuja, as the younger sister, persuading the elder one to relinquish her anger against her husband and the world in general, Gulzar does away with the scenes altogether and finds other situations to set his codas in.

Gulzar admits that, going by Shakespeare's script, there was really 'no scope for songs'. But after *Do Dooni Char*, and keeping in mind the audience preference for musical interludes, he felt that he could clearly see 'a place for one song'. 'Babuji loved songs and wanted them in the film, so we had to think hard. I remonstrated with him, said that the songs were not needed [and] the pace of the comedy would be lost, but he was so keen I could not deny him. I negotiated with HMV. I asked them to create a two-song EP, or Extended Play, record, which were very popular then. But HMV said, "Give us three songs and we will manage. We will do the sound track." I thought a third song was a liability but added it anyway as a scene between husband and wife right at the beginning, before the drama starts.'

The trio of Gulzar, Rahul Dev Burman and Asha Bhosle would make great music together throughout their association. In *Angoor*, they delivered. Both the songs sung by female artists are by Asha and it is to the singer's credit that she oozes sensuality in one and presents the chaste virtuosity of a music student in the other.

The song that Gulzar felt fitted naturally into the story line is '*Roz roz dali dali, kya likhta, bhawara, bawara*', which Deepti Naval sings. It is sung in an auditorium and sets the scene for her first glimpse of the wrong Sanjeev Kumar whom she mistakes for her Jeejaji (brother-in-law). A similar scene in *Do Dooni Char* was preluded by a boisterous group song set in a mela, complete with tightrope walkers, tumble wheels, merry-go-rounds and dancers in folk costumes.

R.D. Burman set the song in a semi-classical mode, using the raga Kalyan as a base.

It has the right mix of ease and difficulty to merit being sung on stage and to justify the statement made earlier that the singer has been rehearsing hard for the show over the past two days. Deepti, as she delivers the song, looks quite the student of music, somewhat nervous but pleased with the command she has over her delivery.

Gulzar's lyrics match the occasion perfectly. Through the symbol of the *bhawara*, or bumble bee, he hints at the singer's single status and subconscious yearning for love – a theme oft repeated in Hindi films. The song by itself, prima facie, is asexual; there is no suggestive phraseology and the lyrics are perfectly in sync with the character of the singer, who is intelligent and well-read enough to choose a song that assigns poetic reasons for the bumble bee's wanderings. That it is a song not written by her is evident in the fact that she refers to her book occasionally.

The lyrics are worth a look:

Roz roz daali daali kya likh jaaye
Bhanwra bawara bawara
Roz roz daali daali kya likh
Jaaye bhanwra bawara
Kaliyo ke naam koi likhe paigaam koi
Kaliyo ke naam koi likhe paigaam koi
Bawara bhanwra bawara
Roz roz daali daali kya likh jaaye
Bhanwra bawara bawara

Bite hue mausam ki koi nishaani hogi
Pa ma pa ma ga ma ga re
Ga ni re ni ma ga re pa
Bite hue mausam ki koi nishaani hogi
Dard purana koi yaad puraani hogi
Dard purana koi yaad puraani hogi
Koi to daastaan hogi naa
Roz roz daali daali kya likh jaaye
Bhanwra bawara bawara

Hoga koi wada hoga wada nibhata hoga
Hoga koi wada hoga wada nibhata hoga
Shaakho pe likh kar yaad dilata hoga
Shaakho pe likh kar yaad dilata hoga
Yaad to aati hi hogi naa

Roz roz daali daali
Roz roz daali daali
Roz roz daali daali kya likh jaaye
Bhanwra bawara bawara.

'*Ho(n)tho(n) pe biti baat aayi hai, vada nibhane ki raat aayi hai*' is the song that Gulzar placed reluctantly at the very start of the story. It could well have been just a song to be enjoyed for its tune but Sanjeev Kumar and Moushumi with their perfect, unerring sense of the mood and timing, manage to convey much more. The entire relationship between the husband and wife, Moushumi's nature, the fact that she does love her husband but loves her jewellery just as much and her expectation from him to keep a promise she has obviously wrested from him is all made clear in the three-and-a-half minutes of the song. Gulzar turned a 'liability' into a well-articulated advantage.

Take the lines:

yaad to hogi kuch bhuli bisari aise barsi thi chand si misari
yaad to hogi kuch bhuli bisari aise barsi thi chand si misari
    chand ko chabane ki
chand ko chabane ki raat aayi hai.

There is the hint of mischief and teasing presented in a poetic, romantic packaging.

Again, in the following stanza, by which time the scene has heated up a little more:

yaad hai us din barish bhi thi chhat bhigi khawish bhi thi
yaad hai us din barish bhi thi chhat bhigi khawish bhi thi
chhat pe jane ki raat aayi hai, chhat pe jane ki raat aayi hai
ho(n)tho(n) pe biti baat aayi hai vada nibhane ki raat aayi hai
ho(n)tho(n) pe biti baat aayi hai

Here you have the perfect blend of Gulzar's poetic genius with the teasing visual of Moushumi, whose seduction has a definite purpose. And so the story moves forward with the next scene, where Ashok 1 swears he will not come home without the necklace.

Perhaps a line about the start of the song is also important here, where RD uses his favoured bass guitar and combines it with different percussion instruments with occasional support from acoustic guitars. To quote from musicalmavericks.blogspot.in: 'Collectively, these sounds enhance the canvas of the song enormously. Another testimony of RD's emphasis and fascination for the sound of a song.'

It is however the remix of the classic '*Pritam aan milo*', which perhaps remains the most interesting song in the film.

The song has an interesting history, if a somewhat sad one. Scored by O.P. Nayyar at a time when he was yet to find his place among the successful music directors of the time, the song's lyrics were written by his wife, Saroj Mohini.

Influenced as he was, like most of his generation, by the semi-classical songs sung by the inimitable K.L.Saigal, Nayyar modelled the orchestration on those sung by the idol and used simple instrumentation, restricting himself to the sitar, tabla and organ. He approached the singer C.H.Atma, who sang in the Saigal style to record the number in his sonorous voice and his old world enunciation heavily influenced by his Punjabi tongue, bringing everything together perfectly. The era was still hung-up on melodious, old style romantic laments in the vein of a mourning Devdas and the song became a huge hit.

'Pritam aan milo' would give O.P. his first big break and C.H. Atma a number of films under O.P.'s baton. And all would have been well but for the fact that times, and audience tastes, were changing.

O.P. Nayyar's semi-classical, sonorous compositions in the super slow mode were rejected, along with the singer who rendered them equally soulfully. An upbeat generation wanted upbeat, frothy songs. A new breeze was blowing in cinema and new voices had made the old seem out of date. C.H. Atma never really recovered his standing and his voice was relegated to the occasional private soirées where nostalgia prevailed for the duration. He would be heard again on screen only in V. Shantaram's *Geet Gaaya*

Pattharon Ne (1964) and later in *Kaamchor* (1982), where the 'old record' of a song actually composed by Rajesh Roshan would be played by the hero to entice his heroine.

O.P. Nayyar himself changed track to add foot-tapping rhythms to his compositions and, though the semi-classical does show up in his compositions in later years, his signature would remain the fast-paced, breezy number. However, he could not resist using '*Pritam aan milo*' in his next big assignment, for Guru Dutt's *Mr. and Mrs. '55* (1955), where he had Geeta Dutt sing the song in a much shorter version.

Gulzar uses the song again in *Angoor*. Its reuse is justified. The semi-urban Ashok 2 would be a typical listener of such songs as his mother might have loved them, so it comes to his mind naturally when he thinks of a code to let Bahadur 2 know that he is at the door.

When the song is finally sung on screen, it fits in wonderfully. Ashok 2 is in a drunken sleep, unable to resist Sudha's efforts at plying him with alcohol. Also, being a non-drinker, he succumbs easily to the narcotic powers of his drink. Tanu and Prema are drugged with bhang-laced pakoras and Bahadur 2, who has also partaken of some, is the first to wake up and seek out his master so they can escape this house where everyone seems either possessed or mad.

He sings the code and when he gets no response, continues surprisingly tunefully to sing the *antara* (the paragraph that follows the first in a song) of the song.

R.D. Burman gives the song a changed, fluctuating tempo, though he keeps the original tune. Gulzar adds his own words. And the song fits in perfectly, as it does manage to draw Ashok 2 out of his sleep and towards Bahadur 2 as easily as a snake charmer's music draws out a snake from its hole. Gulzar changes the original lyrics to keep only the first lines. It was something he would do on many other occasions too, as in '*Chaiya Chaiya Chaiya*' (from Bule Shah's '*Thaiya Thaiya*') and the use of Ghalib's well-known line '*Jee dhondta hai* ' in the song '*Dil dhoondta hai*' for the film *Mausam*.

The new lines fit the scene perfectly. Adding humour to the song, which is supposedly steeped in pathos, Sapan Chakraborty maintains just the right mood with his voice modulation so that, at times, it carries a hint of C.H. Atma's original.

Pritam aan milo pritam aan milo
Ho dukhiya jiwan kaise
Bitaun pritam aan milo

Raat akele dar lagta hai
Jungle jaisa ghar lagta hai
Chhalti hai jab tez hawaye
Leharata hunter lagta hai
Kitne hunter khau
Pritam aan milo

Ho dukhiya jiwan kaise
Bitaun pritam aan milo

Birah me koyi bol raha hai
Pida ka ras ghol raha hai
Phir se jaan labo par aaye
Phir koyi ghunghat khol raha hai
Mukhda kaise chupaun
Pritam aan milo
Ho dukhiya jiwan kaise
Bitaun pritam aan milo

The instrumentation too, is completely suited to the scene. Besides the bass guitar, used only for sounding the 'sa' repeatedly, R.D. Burman made the song both comic and personal by adding sound effects and overlaying the sounds of dogs, frogs, a door opening, the ticking of a clock and the wind. Even galloping horses add to the rhythm, along with a ball that seems to be bouncing up the stairs, keeping with the post-bhang mood.

As important to a film as its action, especially in the suspense or comic genre, is the background music. One has only to watch an Alfred Hitchcock film to realize how the master filmmaker used music to set the hair of his audience on end. The careful blend of instruments, onomatopoeic sounds and silence can speak as loudly as words, and create a mood that takes the viewer back to a time in their childhood when they were alternately fascinated and frightened while listening to ghost stories narrated by an adult.

R.D. Burman uses the background score in such a way that it indicates both humour and suspense alternately, as the situation demands. Playing in tandem with the word-play and the situational comedy, the musical score knits the film closely into a homogenous, continuous whole. The credits roll to a score that blends the modern rhythms to the soft strains of the sitar that follows. It is alternately fast and gentle and changes without notice, giving an intimation of the twists and turns in the story ahead. Most of the time, the dialogues hold centre stage with almost no background music to take away the import of the words. Gulzar and Pancham respect each other's talent enough to give the other the required space without crowding in. So, in the scenes where suspense is paramount and the humour is inherent in the action rather than in dialogue, Pancham takes over to create the mood with background music.

Take the scene where Sudha has led Ashok 2 into the bedroom. She is offering him a drink and is bent on placating him through cajoling and seduction. The music is low in the background, a soft playing of a traditional tune that reminds one of S.D. Burman's melodies. The music stops when Sudha steps aside to respond to Tanu's advice to handle Ashok with care. When the exchange between Sudha and Ashok 2 moves to a suggestive mode with Sudha suggesting he drop his dhoti (and Sudha's love is expressed in the statement that she will not let Ashok out of her sight for even a moment), a flute starts playing, adding a romantic dimension to the background tune. Then the dialogue takes over and the music is stilled.

A much more restrained background music is part of the scene where Ashok 2 is asked to accompany a farm worker who will guide him to the bus stop. The route is lonely and only the sound of birds breaks the silence. When Ashok realizes from the looks of the stranger that he is dressed in the manner of a goon who does not baulk at murder, a suspenseful tune plays briefly then stops to let the dialogue take over.

But the scene which uses background music to its maximum advantage is the one where Bahadur 2 tries to extract the key to the lock on the front door from inside Prema's blouse. The music starts the moment he opens the kitchen door, low but insistent; the repetitive tune with low notes adds just the right amount of tension to the scene. When he sits down to do the dark deed, a pastoral note on the violin adds a lightness, reminding us that this is not a sexual scene but part of a comic sequence. Using the jal tarang or xylophone as punctuations to mark the progress and setbacks of the theft in progress, Pancham takes the story forward by providing a strong support to the visuals. The tune wails in a series of dropping notes as Bahadur pulls on a string that is seemingly endless and is actually not attached to the key but unravelling the blouse; and it lifts to play an urgent tune, repeated till the two make their escape.

Background sounds add their bit: In the early scene when we are first introduced to Ashok 2 and he is reading a thriller in the train, the sound of the train on the sleepers is the only background sound. It is more evident in the textual pauses and the rat-a-tat adds to the suspense of the story Ashok is reading. Entirely engrossed, he adds his own onomatopoeic sound effects, dodging imaginary bullets, and when Bahadur touches his shoulder in perfect sync with the same action occurring in the book, he screams. The train whistles at this point, adding its pitch to Ashok's scream and heightening the mood.

In the scene at the goldsmiths when Ashok 1 has gone to ask for the necklace and Mansoor Mia is explaining that the necklace has already been handed over by him to Ashok in the early hours of the morning, there is only a *tap tap tap* towards the climax of the scene. It adds a heightened sense of suspense to the comedy and is suggestive of a goldsmith tapping lightly with his hammer.

Pancham introduces a *pip pip* sound that sounds a digital alarm in scenes like the one where Tanu accosts Ashok 2 in the foyer. As she approaches Ashok, the alarm sound of *pip pip pip* rising to a crescendo intimates the viewers of trouble ahead and tunes their subconscious to give closer attention to the unfolding scene. All through, Gulzar uses the *pip pip* as a device to alert the audience and elevate interest. Pancham uses great restraint in not adding instruments at this point.

The sound is repeated in the scene in which Mansoor Mia meets Ashok 2 at the rickshaw stand and hands over the necklace to him. The moment Mansoor Mia sights Ashok waiting in the rickshaw and approaches him, the *pip pip* sets up the warning. Audiences now know what to expect. And yet again when Bahadur 1 bargains over the rope he must buy for Sudha to hang herself with and walks away, and Bahadur 2 comes into the scene, the *pip pip* goes off. Further, in the scene where Ashok 2 alights from the bus to catch sight of Ashok 1 buying radishes, the *pip pip* warns us that there is confusion afoot.

Perhaps the most overlooked background sound is the music playing in Tanu's room. The tape recorder is playing a Begum Akhtar ghazal, of which we hear a line of the *antara*, '*Kya ada thi woh jaane nissar ki*'. Of no significance at that point beyond indicating the mood Tanu might have dropped off to sleep in, which is the implication that Bahadur 2 collects from the quick glimpse, the song might just have been Gulzar's way of linking the night to the last scene, where a bewildered Tanu talks about a kiss that she received that night from Ashok 2.

Of such knitted ideas are great comedies made.

chapter twelve

The Song as Comedy

Jest Music

ରେ

This is as good a time as any to introspect a bit and examine the role of funny songs in Hindi cinema.

Songs have been used to evoke laughter since the golden era of Hindi cinema. Sometimes the song is situational, other times it carries a message and, in later years, it became the signature of comedians who could merit screen space all on their own and have songs written for them; Johnny Walker and Mehmood being two such actors who were allotted songs along with the main stars of the films.

Comic songs like '*Aana meri jaan sunday ke sunday*' (*Dulari*, 1947), '*Mere piya gaye rangoon*' (1949) and '*Lara lappa*' (1950), which hint at social scenarios beyond the comic, are still popular today. The tunes and words matched perfectly to uplift the listeners' mood and, besides, they were very hummable songs.

In *Albela*, Bhagwan made an unlikely dancing hero but the story helped add credibility to the role and Bhagwan's own immaculate acting skills and nimble-footedness combined with the sparkle of Geeta Bali helped immortalize the film as well as its songs. C. Ramchandra, the maestro with a flair for light, catchy tunes created a classic comic number with '*Bholi soorat dil ke khote*', which once again had lyrics with societal overtones. The choreography of the song kept the comic element in place; Bhagwan's moves are programmed to keep the mood light and laughter bubbling just under the surface, even as the music sets the foot tapping.

Raj Kapoor and Guru Dutt, contemporaries with very different yet effective approaches to filmmaking, used the comic song in different ways. If '*Mera joota hai Japani*' (*Shree 420*, 1955) helped create empathy for the down at heel vagabond hero who could laugh at himself and evoke our smiles too, Guru Dutt's songs for Johnny Walker in *Mr. and Mrs. '55*, '*Jane kahan mera jigar*', '*Zara hat ke, zara bach ke*' from *C.I.D.*, and *Pyaasa*'s '*Tel malish*' ensured the comedian built up his phalanx of fans, even as the songs created comic relief while taking the story forward. Taking a cue from these directors, good filmmakers in the years ahead would use comic songs to take the story line around yet another corner.

If Mohammad Rafi could give his clear and inimitable voice a comic turn for Johnny Walker, Kishore Kumar was not one to be left behind. His antics in comic roles, where he 'sang' '*CAT cat, cat mane billi*', in *Dilli Ka Thug*, and '*Eena meena deeka*' in *Aasha* (both songs with Asha Bhosle) had already prepared the audience for the time when, in films like *Chalti Ka Naam Gaadi* (1958) and *Funtoosh* (1956), he would sing comic songs. That Kishore could bend his voice to express pathos as beautifully is a given today, but he gave his comic songs an edge with his own facial expressions and body language to match the audio perfectly. '*Hum the, woh thi, aur sama rangeen*' in *Chalti Ka Naam Gaadi* is a perfect example of the wonderful synergy of body and voice rhythms. Kishore's funny songs were often just that; a bit of whimsy, a moment of pure fun. Add Asha and Madhubala to the mix and you have the outrageously creative rib tickler sung perfectly, as in this song from *Chalti Ka Naam Gaadi*:

Mai sitaaron ka taraanaa, mai bahaaron ka fasaanaa
Leke ik angdaai mujh pe, daal nazar ban ja diwaanaa

Mai sitaaron ka taraanaa, mai bahaaron ka fasaanaa
Leke ik angdaai mujh pe, daal nazar ban ja diwaanaa

Roop ka tum ho khazaanaa, tum ho meri jaan ye maanaa
Lekin pahale de do meraa, paach rupaiyaa baaraa aanaa
Paanch rupaiyaa, baaraa aanaa-aaaa
Maaregaa bhaiyaa, naa naa naa naa-aaaa

Maal zar, bhulkar, dil jigar humse nishaani maango naa
Dilrubaa, kya kahaa, dil jigar kya hai jawaani maango naa
Tere liye majnu ban saktaa hun
Lailaa lailaa kar saktaa hun
Chaahe namunaa dekh lo haay
Khun-e-dil pine ko aur laqt-e-jigar khaane ko
Khun-e-dil pine ko aur laqt-e-jigar khaane ko
Ye gizaa milti hai lailaa
Ye gizaa milti hai lailaa
Tere diwaane ko
Tere diwaane ko

O ho ho josh-e-ulfat kaa zamaanaa, laage hai kaisaa suhaanaa
Leke ik angdaai mujh pe, daal nazar ban jaa diwaanaa...

The tune ranges from the light fantastic to the sincerely classical. The vision on screen is fantasy-tinged with a real despair but it is in Majrooh Sultanpuri's lyrics that the song's comic worth is revealed.

Manna Dey got his share of comic songs as Mehmood came into his own as an actor who commanded songs as part of his screen space. In *Ziddi* (1964), Mehmood sings '*Main tere pyaar mein kya kya na bana dilbar*' with Shobha Khote lip-syncing to Geeta Dutt's voice. Though only faintly funny, the comedian still evoked laughs with the song. But he took the comic song to the next level with numbers like '*Hum kaale hain to kya hua*' in *Gumnaam* and the 'Haanji' transgender song in *Kunwara Baap*, starting, perhaps, the downward slide of lyrics and body language in the history of comic songs.

However, one classic number that Mehmood has to his credit is the duet with Sunil Dutt alias Kishore Kumar in *Padosan*. The blend of classical styles, the rib tickling lyrics and the impeccable rendition by both singers of a complex tune created by R.D. Burman, layered on visuals that carry their own quotient of mirth, make it a song that surpasses the best in *Chalti Ka Naam Gaadi*; a feat that has never been equalled.

Yet the history of comic songs in Hindi films cannot be complete without a mention of the funny numbers with I.S. Johar and Pran.

Pran, surprisingly, for he could do a great comic turn, is remembered mainly for two comic numbers. One from *Munimji* (1955), where in the song '*Dil ki umangein hai jawan*', he creates a situation where the audience enjoys the fact that he is being made a fool of and coaxed to sing though he has no ear for music, and the second in *Victoria No. 203* (1972), where, with Ashok Kumar, he not only essayed the comic to perfection but sang the duet '*Hum do deewane dil ke*'.

And though I.S. Johar has many comic roles and songs to his credit, including the *Bewaqoof* number where he substitutes for the radio, singing in many voices, it is the Rafi-Manna Dey number in *Shagird* – '*Bade mian deewane*' – that sticks in public memory.

Om Prakash in *Buddha Mil Gaya* (1971), singing '*Aayo kahan se nandalal*' is not really comic, but the audience perceives it as comedy because it knows that every rendition of the song is followed by a murder.

Though directors like Hrishikesh Mukherjee and films like *Gol Maal* and *Satte Pe Satta* (1982) kept humour in musical interludes squeaky clean with songs like '*Gol maal hai bhai sab gol maal hai*' and '*Pyar hume kis mod pe le aaya*', the tide was turning.

The 1990s came with a lowered bar for humour, where songs were rather bawdier than comic. Suggestive words, crude body language and slapdash tunes made the front row audience clap and whistle but it was a far cry from the sophisticated and subtle comedy of the songs from the 1960s and 1970s.

Yo Yo Honey Singh's '*Char bottle vodka*' for *Ragini MMS* (2011), and '*Khada hai*' from *Andaaz* (1994) are enough to illustrate the downward direction taken by comedy in songs. And, sadly, even actors of the stature of Anil Kapoor and Juhi Chawla seem unable to desist from descending to the depths of bad taste.

Clean, happy and poetic, *Angoor*'s three songs hold their own in this chart and can evoke a smile from any listener who has watched the film, even today.

chapter thirteen

Angoor

The Film

ॐ

'Gulzar works very quietly on his scripts. He does not tom-tom them but when it is ready, he produces it and presents it.' Deepti Naval has vivid memories of *Angoor*. 'He read the complete script to us, two or three of us were present, and we were all charged by the whole idea.'

Gulzar was very clear about his cast. 'I was signed up along with Haribhai Jariwala (Sanjeev Kumar),' Moushumi remembers. 'I was close to him. I was perhaps the only one who called him Zari and he would laugh at that. He called me one evening and said, "Gulzar will come to you for his next film, ask your terms. No one can do it except you."' Moushumi knew Gulzar, 'He used to come home to teach my mother-in-law Urdu. He spoke to my husband and dropped in. I knew it was a big budget film and said yes at once.' Moushumi had also interacted with the director when he had worked with Hemant Kumar, her father-in-law, in *Khamoshi*, for which he wrote the songs. Moushumi remembers that it was a lot of fun doing the film. 'Haribhai told Gulzar, "She has understood the role," so Gulzar said very little to me about how to interpret it.'

Gulzar is very clear on why he took on Moushumi for the role. 'She is so bubbly even in real life. I had been watching her from her first film, *Balika Badhu* (1967) in Bangla. She would come from school and go straight for rehearsal. And she was full of mischief, even then. I liked her spontaneity and thought it would work wonderfully for the role of Sudha in *Angoor*.'

Moushumi also talks about her approach to the role. 'I would do it spontaneously and sit back. I was a one-take actress. Ask me to redo it for a second take and I would get self-conscious. I would give my take and say, "*Chalo, ho gaya*." Gulzar called me "the laziest actress" he had worked with but he trusted me. He knew me since the time I used to wear frocks.'

Gulzar had one problem to cope with while working with Moushumi on *Angoor*: the actress was pregnant with her second daughter. 'We had to take many long, long shots, as I was visibly pregnant,' Moushumi remembers. Otherwise, her director had no issues. 'She is an actress who becomes the role. I don't think there is any role in which she has failed. She never took her career seriously or she would have gone really far,' is his reading of Moushumi.

Moushumi also has happy memories of working with Deepti Naval, a 'very sweet girl'. She remembers that Gulzar was very upset with her and said something sharp, which made her cry. 'They did not dare tell me anything,' she says of her directors, including Gulzar. 'I would give it back saying either you convince me or let me do it my way. I concentrate on what I am doing. Moushumi knew everyone in the film. Deven Verma was 'half Bengali' and a friend, and all the production people knew her, including the cameraman, so 'despite the tight schedules, it was a fun film to do.'

Gulzar admits to problems with Deepti. 'Her presence was very good, and she made the perfect contrast to Moushumi, but she was too academic. She would want to script out the dialogues and how to say them and work out movements ... It was not my way of working.'

Deepti speaks with admiration of just this quality in Gulzar. 'Gulzar is a writer of precision. He had a metre in mind, the rhythm of a sentence in his brain. He knew exactly how a dialogue should be delivered, whether it would end on a high note or a low one. He was strict about it and the only person who could improvise on it was Sanjeev Kumar, who would do so but without changing the inherent structure and rhythm of the line.' According to her, 'Gulzar would read a scene, then communicate the general essence of what he wants from you. As he read, one could understand the timing of it and how to interpret it.' Perhaps because they had not worked together before, Gulzar would explain to Deepti in detail. Deepti remembers one particular moment in his directing her. 'He wanted me to drop my jaw in surprise. When I did it, it was so typically an American movement that of course it did not work. He was too self-conscious to demonstrate what it was he wanted, told me "an open jaw look will do" and continued to make me redo it till he was satisfied.'

Gulzar worked hard on the little gestures that would typify and personalize his characters, making them real. He admits having had to work doubly hard with Deepti on these little gestures. 'I wanted her glasses to slip down her nose and for her to push them up with a wrinkle of her nose ... People who wear glasses typically do that. But it was very difficult to get her to get it right. Finally, she did but it was still not as perfect as I wanted it.'

Deepti gives her director full marks for adding natural touches to scenes. She mentions the scene where Moushumi is washing her eyes in an eyeglass as she continues her conversation as an example. 'It is so natural and adds a realism to the scene without any effort. The film reveals itself and its characters through such scenes, and everyone joins in the enjoyment.'

Gulzar was very clear even as he was writing *Angoor* that his 'two anchors' Hari (Sanjeev Kumar) and Pancham would be an intrinsic part of the film. There was no scope for music but the film could not be done without Pancham. And when HMV demanded three songs that they hoped to combine with the dialogues into an album, Pancham's presence was justified.

Talking about his favourite music director, Gulzar goes back into memories of their good times together.

'I met Pancham for the first time when I was doing '*Mora gora ang laile*'. He was a chubby boy in knickers and would come carrying his *dagga* under his arm and give rhythm at the sittings.' Somehow, despite their age difference, a friendship grew between the two. Gulzar 'used to meet him at Jet. It was a building at the end of a long, empty road. Those days, there was nothing except a football ground between National College and his house. Every time I would meet him, he would say, "Go upstairs and meet Baba," meaning his father, S.D. Burman. I would dutifully do so. I do not know why he said that. Perhaps, in his mind, he did not like me being pushed out of the film (*Bandini*) after that one song. I think he liked my song and thought I deserved to write more lyrics for his father.

'Over the years, the friendship grew into a creative partnership. He was spontaneous. He would come with a thali with five or six bowls of *phirni*, which he had made, placed on them like a puja offering and say, "*Chalo*, let us go." And we would go to Filmalaya, where he had a recording. Sometimes we just drove around. I think we never really had a formal sitting to make songs. His songs would happen while we were chatting between his recordings or driving. My best work was done with him.

'He had tunes, so many of them; they rose spontaneously to his mind. And he had visions. He would say, "I can see Didi's face. She must sing this song." Or it would be Asha, or Kishore. Sometimes he would say, "Gulzar, this is yours, *tera thobda samne aajata hai.* Your face is coming in front of my eyes."

'And often, after a recording, when Asha was also in the studio, he would say, "*Chal yaar, yeh faltu kaam tere ghar pe ja ke kartein hain.*" That is how *Dil Padosi Hai* happened. To fit in the songs that have no place in films ... Films don't give you enough scope to write. Like the song "*Raat Christmas ki* " in *Dil Padosi Hai.* It is about two people at a Christmas party, both already committed but attracted to each other. Working together on such tunes and songs was what our friendship was about. It transcended work.' Gulzar still owns the harmonium that his friend used to play on to compose his tunes or work on them.

Equally certain that his film needed Sanjeev Kumar in the lead double role, Gulzar wrote the film with the actor in mind. The relationship between them stretches back to before either of them had entered the world of films. 'I was with IPTA; he was with INT[7]. We used to meet at rehearsals at Bhulabhai. He was keen on entering films and was taking acting lessons from P.D. Shenoy, who was head of the acting

---

7   IPTA or Indian People's Theatre Association; INT or Indian National Theatre

school which Leela Chitnis' son and Joy Mukherjee also attended, among others. P.D. was also a director. I knew him.'

Gulzar remembers an incident from that time. 'They were rehearsing a play and I ran into Hari standing outside, looking very happy. Obviously, some Gujarati woman had said, "Joy *sarika dikhta hai*; he looks like Joy." He was delighted and told me this, adding, "*Apna bhi chance to hai*". To him, it translated as a chance to get a break in films.'

Gulzar worked with Sanjeev Kumar for the first time in *Sunghursh*. Abrar Alvi had left the film, so Gulzar was called in. 'The film was based on the short story "*Layli Asmaner Ayna*" by Mahasweta Devi. They felt "Bengali *aadmi hai* and story Bengali *hai*. Gulzar can do it." The script was in a huge mess when I got in. Dilip sahib had written in large portions, he used to do that, and the novel itself was so huge that only portions of it could be used. There were a lot of discussions before we could finalize the script and structure. Sanjeev had been taken for the film.'

Gulzar remembers the first scene Sanjeev shot. It was a game of *shatranj* (chess). 'He had a dialogue, "*Chaal to hum chal chuke*" (I have already made my moves), and I remember Dilip sahib's reaction to it. He was clearly impressed. He asked Rawail, the producer, "Where did you find this actor?" And Rawail replied, "In theatre."'

If in *Angoor*, Sanjeev plays a man close to his real age, it was a rare departure from the roles Gulzar assigned him in his other films. 'Once, I told him, "*Bus kar,* stop playing old men in films," and he said, "Look who's talking." True enough, I did age him in most of my films and the younger bits came only in flashbacks.' Perhaps Gulzar was subconsciously influenced in this by the fact that he had seen a twenty-three-year-old Sanjeev Kumar playing the father in the Hindi version of *All My Sons* (1947), with Manavendra Chitnis, who was about the same age, playing one of his sons. The acting had been so real; the actor had copied the mannerisms of the aged so exactly and recreated the persona on the stage so effectively that even Prithviraj Kapoor, who was in the audience, was impressed enough to ask who had played the role.' He asked Sanjeev this question, not realizing that it was he who had played the part on stage,' Gulzar recollects. 'Yes, that image stuck with me. I knew he was one actor who could carry both old and young roles in the same film convincingly. It is not at all easy.'

For such an actor, a double role with quiet nuances to tell the difference between the two was, of course, easy.

Sanjeev Kumar starred in most of Gulzar's films, from *Parichay* (1972) and *Koshish* (1972) to *Angoor* and beyond, and Gulzar's friendship with him was a close one. 'Hari loved food. He loved eating non-vegetarian food and would tell my sister, who lived with me those days, "I will come to have chicken." To me, he would say, "I will come anytime. I need Black Label. If you cannot afford it, I will leave a bottle here with you." And, sure enough, he would drop in any time after a shoot, often without warning. And I would wake my sister up so she could cook something for him.'

On the sets, Sanjeev endeared himself with his natural sense of humour. 'He was a natural; perfect for a comic role,' according to Gulzar. 'He was a favourite with the girls too. They laughed at his dress sense. He would wear a bright yellow tie [and] they would help him dress better; get things for him to wear. Yet his late-coming would irk everyone. I remember, on the sets of *Namkeen* (1982), Sharmila, Shabana and Waheeda ganged up on him over his constant late-coming. "We get stale by the time he comes, so we have decided not to talk to him," they told me. When Hari came, he sensed immediately [that] something was wrong. I pretended not to have noticed and set up his shot. Once the shot was over, the anger vanished. They hugged him and told him they had decided not to talk to him, but his acting was too good and they could not stay angry with him.'

With Sanjeev Kumar, Gulzar would read the entire scene, rehearse it once and start shooting it. Then he would leave it open for him to take it to the next level. 'He had the ability to take simple lines and add so much humour into them with a pause, or an inflection, that I needed to say nothing more to him. The scene would be perfect.'

Talking about a scene from an earlier film *Parichay*, Gulzar recollects how he shot the song '*Beeti na bitaiyi raina*'.

'It was a one-shot take and he joins in the song in the middle of a line. He comes down the steps and takes up the song, and does it so naturally ... I don't know many other actors who could do this so effortlessly. I was so impressed, I told him, "Ask what you want, *jo mango doonga*." He said, "Will you? For sure?" I thought what (sic) he want? He and Sharmila made plans often to watch films after schedule and I thought he might want *chhutti*. But he said, "Paan *chod do*." I enjoyed paan, liked a bit of *kimam* now and then, and had never guessed he hated the habit. I gave up paan from that day. Such was our friendship.

'He was a true friend and, whether we were working together or not, we kept connected.'

Sanjeev Kumar left memories with others in *Angoor* too. 'Haribhai was a foodie and he would insist I get food on the sets,' Moushumi recounts. 'Often, he would call to say, "Cook *ko bol do, main khana khake jaoonga aur* non-veg *khana*."'

He was a habitual late-latif, Moushumi remembers, and would say, 'Unless I am prepared, I won't leave the make-up room.' And he disregarded all her scoldings. 'He would come at 12 for a 9 a.m. shift, unlike Jeetendra, who would come early. I, too, would be at the studio at 6 and get my make-up done *araam se*, drinking tea in the meantime. I hated going to the sets all made-up,' Moushumi adds. Also sharp in her memory is the fact that Sanjeev and Deven Verma made a loveable duo, the 'blessed duo' had a 'good *rishta*' which vibed wonderfully through the film and the scenes between them 'sparkled'.

Deepti Naval says of Deven Verma that he was a natural and that his humour was sophisticated, adding that he was her mother's 'favourite actor'. But Gulzar has the best description for the actor who won the Filmfare Award for his roles in *Angoor*. 'He was a humourist who excelled at comedy.'

At the end of a discussion on some aspects of how he conceived the salient points of *Angoor* as a director comes this typical Gulzar gem. 'I decided to name the characters in *Angoor* on the stars of *Bhranti Bilash*. Thus, Tanu and Sudha, and so on.'

chapter fourteen

Dialogue as Comedy

A Smile in Every Line

క్ర

Apart from *Chupke Chupke* (1975), which came later, *Angoor* is perhaps the best example of Gulzar's ability to use words to evoke a smile or even loud laughter. However, knowing that the film will be watched by all levels of audience, these words combine with many other devices to create a humorous whole.

Repetition, putting stress on words, using common phrases to illustrate a situation or event, turning a line on its head to mean something quite different or a kind of pun and introducing subsidiary characters who add a physical as well as a verbal humour to the main plot are the main devices used by the writer-director in *Angoor*. It holds together mainly because each line and sentence has been written with a poet's economy and knowledge of the weightage of words.

Angoor uses situation and dialogue in tandem, setting the tone of the scene with the former and adding the punches with the latter.

Thus, in the early scene introducing Ashok 1, his wife and his sister-in-law, he has Ashok 1 kicking his feet under the table and encountering his sister-in-law's feet, which he believes is his wife's, even though her feet are tucked safely under her where she's sitting cross-legged on the chair. This is in order to avoid the fallout of his habit of playing toesy toesy. In this way, the characters get established and the relationships between them are indicated. The punch comes when Tanu says, '*Jijaji yeh mere pair hain, didi ke nahin*' (These are my feet, not Didi's), and Ashok 1 asks, '*Phir didi ke pair kahan hain?*' (Then where are Didi's feet?). To this, Tanu counters, '*Biwi kahiye, didi to meri hain*' (Call her your biwi [wife]. She is my Didi [sister]).

Further on, at the end of the same scene, Gulzar uses another subtle device to hint at the theme of the film, when Sudha says she has got in her hand, '*Do badshah, do gulam*', adding, '*Main to tang aagayi hoon in duplicaton se*' (Two kings, two knaves. I am sick of these duplicates). Little does she know what the rest of the day has in store for her – in double measure.

Duplication of thought as a device occurs repeatedly in the script. When Ashok 2 encounters Bahadur 1 buying radishes in the bazaar, he mistakes him for his own servant, berates him and sends him packing. On returning to the hotel, he accosts Bahadur 2 and demands to know why he was buying radishes in the market instead of guarding the money in the room. Naturally, Bahadur 2 denies all he is accused of and swears that he never left the room. The punch line comes in quietly when he adds that he has ordered radish parathas for lunch. Ashok 2's expression does the rest.

Repetition is an extension of this concept; it serves to endorse an idea in the audience's mind or evoke emotions. Thus, when Girdharilal, the diamond merchant, insists on getting his payment by 11 a.m., it is, at first, funny in the way he delivers the lines, then through repetition at regular intervals in variations on the theme of eleven o'clock. The irritation the others in the scene feel is communicated to the audience, who find themselves responding in a similar fashion yet cannot resist the humour of the situation.

Perhaps the most effective use of this device of repetition is when Bahadur 2 comes into the bedroom with the spiked pakoras and Ashok 2 has just been told by Sudha that Bahadur 1 is going to be a father soon, as Prema is pregnant. Ashok 2's repeated questioning of his servant on how he could father a child so fast, and other such related posers, interspersed with a series of instructions from Bahadur on how best to use the spiked pakoras to send Sudha to sleep, makes for a scene with a high comedy quotient that uses only words to create both suspense and humour.

Linking words with different meanings is another device that is effectively used to make the audience smile at times.

When Ashok 2 is reading aloud from his thriller and imagines that there is someone hiding in the bathroom of his compartment, he challenges the unseen assailant with '*Dekho Dekho, mai ghabrane wala nahin hoon. Main pachaas* novel *padh chuka hoon. Mera matlab hai ki main pachaas goliyaan kha chuka hoon*' (Look, I am not scared. I have read fifty novels. I mean, I have faced fifty bullets). Bahadur 2, who is cowering in mock bravado behind his master, suddenly remembers to ask him, '*Aaj* vitamin *ki goli khaee ki nahin?*' (Did you have your vitamin tablets today or not?).

Gulzar also uses the device of enlisting the audience as an enlightened watcher, almost a co-conspirator, as he leads his characters deeper into the maze of confusion.

Thus, when Tanu mistakes Ashok 2 as her brother-in-law and tells him that she has spent two months preparing for the evening and it was absolutely necessary for him to be present, Ashok 2 thinks she is referring to the gang's plan to rob him and says so in an aside. The audience is privy to both the real issue and the confusion in Ashok's mind, and cannot help but feel amused and smug at the same time.

Using familiar phrases that link the viewers to situations that they have encountered in life or which take them back to their childhood adds an edge to the dialogue and makes sense to the younger set of viewers too.

When Bahadur 2 hears a knock on the door of Ashok 1's house, where he and his master are 'held captive', he imagines that the gang is outside. He approaches the door to check who it is, mumbling '*Jal tum jalal tu, ayee bala ko taal tu*' under his breath, a charm grandmas teach children to use to ward off fear and possible harm.

And again, when Ashok 2 asks for directions to the police station, the man who guides him gives him a bewildering series of rights and left turns that confuse and enrage him – a situation many in the audience who have sought directions to a new place might be familiar with.

And when Ashok 2 says, '*Lagta hai* gang *ne charon taraf se gher liya hai*' (Looks like the gang has surrounded us from all sides), the spoofy quality of that statement cannot help but hit home.

And then, the master wordsmith turns entire phrases on their heads. So it is Ashok 2 who talks about being a victim of his *izzat* being looted, a phrase which heroines usually use in films.

Of course, not all the humour is literary in content. Mansoor Mia brings us laughter with his witticisms like '*Sone ka bhav bhi biwion ki mizaj ki tarhah chadta ja raha hai*' (The price of gold is rising too like the tempers of wives), or his constant hint at diabolic liaisons like when he asks, '*Kis par pagal ho gaye?*' (Who did you get mad over?) when Bahadur 1 states that his master has gone mad. Mansoor's statements like '*Aji chodye hazrat, biwi ke liye bhi koi itni utavli main haar banata hain?*' (Let it be! Who goes off to make a necklace for one's wife in such restlessness?), followed by '*Biwi to barah mahine mein baasi ho jati hain, koi saali waali nahin hain unki?*' (A wife becomes stale in twelve months; there must be a sister-in-law?), is enough to get the gallery slapping their thighs in appreciation.

Playing on the *saali-adhi gharwali* theme common in north Indian concepts of forbidden liaisons, Gulzar has an unknown watcher in the club scene also exclaim that he understands the fracas between Tanu and Ashok 2, and it is because '*Saali aadhi gharwali banne ki koshish main hain*' (The sister-in-law is trying to be half a wife).

And this discussion cannot be complete without a mention of the jewel of a scene in the bedroom where Sudha and Ashok 2 engage in a dialogue with one seducing and the other wary as a cat on a hot tin roof. The use of the concept of nakedness, with a seductive Sudha prancing around the world naked, using terms that denote nakedness euphemistically without mentioning it, and the demure, abashed Ashok 2 blatantly using the word *nanga*, is a fine study in juxtaposition of contrasts in character mood and word usage. Subtle yet effective, it is the device of a master craftsman.

Other examples, like Ashok saying that if Mansoor can call thighs as *jambs*, he can call Ashok Kumar by Kishore

Kumar's name; and the statement that with so many doubles around, the lost mother could also come in duplicate are other classic examples of a sheathed wit, sharp as a barb.

Of course, the punch to the entire film comes with Gulzar's acknowledgement to his inspiration. The Bard meets his modern twentieth-century audience head on, shares a wink and a confidence, and lets the audience take home the package to ruminate over and recall, or retell to renewed bouts of merriment.

This sweet-sour meal delights and, like good grape, mellows into fine wine with the passage of time!

Epilogue

ରେ

Shakespeare went back to the stage when *Angoor* metamorphosed as *Chakkar Chalaye Ghanchakkar*, with the stage play being directed by Salim Arif. Mohammad Zeeshan Ayub played Sanjeev Kumar's part, while Lubna Salim and Shruti Seth played the two co-stars. The title of the play harks back to the opening line of a song in *Do Dooni Char* written by Gulzar.

Swanand Kirkire who played Deven Verma's role jumped into the part, because 'I loved *Angoor*, we all love it, and I had seen the film so many times.' He admits it was a difficult role to translate on stage, especially since he had to remember the transitions between one twin and the other. The changes were quick and came hard on the heels of each other, so 'I had to remember who wore the *kara*, and who did not, and play the part accordingly, too. Of course there was offstage help, but it was on us actors to hold on to our dual roles. The director depended on us to do so.'

The play was a month-and-a-half into rehearsal before it opened to full houses in Mumbai. 'We could do so many more shows, but juggling dates with so many actors is tough,' Arif says.

Gulzar played his part in making the play come alive. Swanand remembers with admiration that Gulzar would read portions from the dialogue, and often correct the cast, ensuring the intonations were perfect.

Some scenes from the film were edited out as being unsuited for the stage, but the story of *Chakkar Chale Ghanchakkar*, the play, remains the same. Quintessentially Gulzar!

Bibliography

ℭ

Print sources

Bhattacharya, Rinki. 2009. *Bimal Roy: The Man Who Spoke in Pictures*. New Delhi: Penguin Viking.

Bichu, Mandar V., 'Preetam Aan Milo', *Cinema Sangeet*, http://www.cinemasangeet.com/hindi-film-music/down-melody-lane/preetam-aan-milo.html, accessed on 17 December 2018.

Eraly, Abraham. 2011. *The First Spring the Golden Age of India*. UK: Penguin Viking.

Jhanvi, S. n.d. 'No Laughing Matter'. *Lights Action Camera.*

Moila, Robert S., and Philip Kolin (eds). 1997. *Critical Essays*. New York, London: Psychology Press, Garland Publishing Inc.

Narwekar, Sanjit. 2005. *Eena Meena Deeka: The Story of Hindi Film Comedy*. Delhi: Rupa & Co.

Other sources

www.rsc.org.uk, for the stage history of *The Comedy of Errors* from the time Shakespeare wrote it to the present day.

www.william-shakespeare.info, for William Shakespeare's *The Comedy of Errors*.

www.shakespearetheatre.org, for the information on Sadler Wells theatre production of *The Comedy of Errors*.